Finding It

And Satisfying My Hunger for Life

Without Opening the Fridge

VALERIE BERTINELLI

Free Press

NEW YORK   LONDON   TORONTO   SYDNEY

Free Press
A Division of Simon & Schuster, Inc.
1230 Avenue of the Americas
New York, NY 10020

First Free Press hardcover edition October 2009

FREE PRESS and colophon are trademarks of Simon & Schuster, Inc.

For information about special discounts for bulk purchases,
please contact Simon & Schuster Special Sales at
1-866-506-1949 or business@simonandschuster.com

The Simon & Schuster Speakers Bureau can bring authors to your live event.
For more information or to book an event contact the Simon & Schuster Speakers Bureau at
1-866-248-3049 or visit our website at www.simonspeakers.com.

Manufactured in the United States of America

1 3 5 7 9 10 8 6 4 2

Library of Congress Cataloging-in-Publication Data
Bertinelli, Valerie,
Finding it : and satisfying my hunger for life without opening the fridge / Valerie Bertinelli.
p. cm.
1. Bertinelli, Valerie, 2. Television actors and
actresses—United States—Biography. I. Title.
PN2287.B4379A3 2009
791.4502'8092—dc22
[B] 2009027256

ISBN 978-1-4391-4163-2
ISBN 978-1-4391-5909-5 (ebook)

To Tom
for finding me

I may change a few words in it here and there before it is finished,
But at the end it's still "Amen."

—Raymond Pettibon

Contents

Part One: Faith

CONTENTS

Part Two: Belief

Finding It

Notes to Myself

Get tomatoes and fruit at the grocery store. Olives, too.

Pick up Tom at the airport at 2 p.m.

Figure out the rest of my life. (Can I do that in thirty minutes?)

Walk at least ten thousand steps. (Continue figuring out my life if necessary.)

"Be who you are and say what you feel because those who mind don't matter and those who matter don't mind."—Theodore Seuss Geisel (Dr. Seuss).

Don't you just love that man?

Introduction

I shouldn't have been offended when my boyfriend Tom walked in on me and commented on my underwear. But I was. Most women would agree—and may even have had the same conversation. I was cleaning out my dresser drawers as I packed for a weekend trip to Laguna Beach for my forty-ninth birthday. Tom came in and began sifting through a pile of t-shirts, bras, and underwear that I put on the bed in a "discard" pile. Without asking what I was doing, he jumped into the middle of the process and came up holding a pair of skin-colored panties as if they were fresh roadkill.

"I hope you aren't going to bring these to the beach," he said.

"As a matter of fact, no, I wasn't," I said. "They're being thrown out, along with everything else in that pile." Still, I was curious what he had against them, a perfectly nice pair of underwear.

"What's wrong with them?" I asked.

"They're granny panties," he said.

Granny panties? I gave him a look that said, "Oh, really, buster. You think so?" I had just spent nearly two years having lost 40 pounds; actually a little more at this time. I hadn't gone through that effort to cover my rear end in drapes. My underwear drawer included bikini-style panties, sheer panties, white panties, black panties, a couple of pastel-colored panties, panties whose lines weren't visible through pants, panties I wore to business meetings, panties I wore when I worked out, panties I wore on special occasions, and panties that said I was in the mood. I had panties for nearly every occasion. The one thing I didn't have were granny panties.

I grabbed the pair in question from Tom. I studied them for a second or two and decided he had no idea what he was talking about.

"These are bikini-style, but with a wider waistband," I explained. "If I had them on, you could still see my belly button."

"V, I'm going to tell you something," he said. "I hope you don't take offense at hearing it. But you've had some nasty underwear, and these are at the top of the list."

"Oh. My. God," I said, tossing the undies back in the throw-out pile. "You don't know what you're talking about."

"Quite the contrary," he said. "I'm a guy. I know about women's underwear."

A dozen different responses came to mind, none of them nice. I chose a response that is rarely part of my repertoire: I bit my tongue and said nothing. I knew Tom's theory about women's underwear was typical of most men. It consisted of grand expectations (my undies were supposed to be chosen for his pleasure, not my convenience or comfort), disappointment (they could never be small enough), and something I'll call "lack-of-string theory"— basically, they increased in size with age until they got so large that women needed the local fire department's hook and ladder brigade to pull them up (not true of mine in any way, shape, or size, thank you very much!).

I have a different take. I think that the slingshot-sized thongs that Tom and most men think of as ideal are thoroughly uncomfortable. After a few men walk around with what is essentially a string of dental floss up their butt all day, I would gladly talk to them about women's underwear. That said, panties *are* a fairly accurate indicator of the way a woman feels about herself.

As Tom would find out once we got to Laguna, I was feeling pretty good about myself.

In many ways, I was better than ever. Just a month earlier, I had let the world see me in a bikini. I'd shot a commercial and a magazine cover, wearing for the first time what I had not dared put on in almost thirty years. I was a little uncomfortable showing that much skin, but, hey, I'd worked my butt off getting in shape, so why not show off a little?

But getting in a bikini was only part of the story. There was so much more that people couldn't see because the transformation had taken place on the inside, deep down in the gooey center. When I saw myself on the cover of *People* magazine, I noticed glimpses of it in my eyes. Granted, most people weren't looking there. But I saw a light and an alive-ness and a renewed hunger for life that hadn't been there since I was a kid, back before I'd eaten my way through life's challenges, insecurities, fears, and disappointments.

I was serious when I said, "I can't believe I did it." But I was talking about more than just fitting into a bikini.

Losing forty pounds was an accomplishment, and getting into a bikini was the exclamation point to all that effort. But anyone who has lost weight—and kept it off—knows that shedding pounds is only the first step in the much bigger and longer project of transformation. But I hadn't known this. Why? I had never kept the weight off.

Over the years, I had gone on more diets than I could count or even remember. Every one of them had worked. I had lost weight. But up till now, I had always failed to keep it off. I'm not alone here. Millions of people know what I'm talking about. Everyone who has gone on a diet knows how to lose weight. All of us are very good at it. The problem is, few of us know how to keep it off. According to the research I found, between 92 and 95 percent of those who lose weight on a diet end up regaining every one of those pounds, and sometimes a few more, within five years. That's insane. It's a problem. And it begs the question, what are we doing wrong?

I thought about this after I reached my weight-loss goal and announced to those following my progress that I was transitioning to maintenance. Then, I woke up that next day and the day after and on days after those and asked myself, What does that mean, maintenance?

One day, I said to myself, "Holy crap! I've been here before and messed up. What had I done wrong? What do I have to do differently this time to keep the weight off?"

Well, as far as I'm concerned, this is the part of weight loss that no one ever talks about: the reality of keeping it off. I think the reason why so many of us have always gained back our weight after months of hard work, self-discipline, and sweat is that we don't know what to do once we hit our goal. We aren't given this crucial information.

I want to change that. Having lost 40 pounds and kept it off for a year, I have figured some things out and acquired some wisdom and insight that I wish I had known as I set out on my weight-loss journey, starting with one fact: Above and beyond all else, losing weight and maintenance are two completely different endeavors.

I had assumed that switching gears from losing weight to maintenance simply meant watching what I ate and exercising daily, but in a more relaxed mode. I was wrong. Maintaining this new, slimmer, healthier version of myself required even more work. Harder work, too.

Talk about a shock!

Talk about a revelation!

When I looked at this new, thinner version of myself, the one who had reached her goal by losing 40 pounds, the one who was supposedly ready to change gears into maintenance, I realized that I wasn't finished. Inside, I didn't feel finished. As it turned out, I wasn't.

Who knew?

I didn't. As I said, on previous diets, I had always lost weight and then regained it plus some extra. I had never been able to keep it off. I would hit my goal, give myself a few days of leniency for good behavior, maybe reward myself with a treat or two and, before I knew it, the weight was piling back on.

This time I vowed not to let that happen to me. However, after losing weight in front of the world, I didn't want to go through the humiliation of regaining it in front of world. I shuddered at the thought of going into the supermarket and seeing the headlines, "Valerie Bertinelli Fat Again." I didn't want to disappoint myself, either.

That was the real issue. I looked good, I felt great, and most important I was learning to like myself more and more. I didn't want to lose any of that. In fact, as I discovered, I wanted to keep going! I couldn't believe it. Losing weight was an eye-opener—a game-changer, as they say on the sports channels.

Losing weight was merely the beginning of a process, and I needed to get in sync with that reality and act accordingly. In other words, by dieting, I had only fixed one problem, my weight. To maintain it, I had to work on everything else—all the things that had made me get fat in the first place.

For me, maintenance became not an effort to keep my weight the same but a daily effort to continue to evolve and grow and work at becoming my best self. Since I began, I have found it exciting, frustrating, challenging, confusing, and ultimately the most rewarding project I have tackled. It should be. It's my life!

In this book, I talk about some of the busiest, hardest, and best days of my life. My teenage son, Wolfie, fell in love; Tom's four wonderful children became more involved in our life together; my mom battled a serious illness; and on top of everything, I worked my butt off (literally) to get into bikini shape for a new Jenny Craig marketing campaign—as if, at age forty-eight, I needed that additional test.

Without knowing any better until I dived in, I needed it more than I realized. It took me to the next level, and along the way I was able to look at the big issues in my life, including family, career, health, friendship, and faith. Though I wasn't always clear about what I believed, my definition of maintenance came to include a deeper sense of faith, a closer relationship with God, and an attempt to find a sense of peace and comfort.

In many ways, the problems I have had to confront sound like a season's worth of plots on a family sitcom. But I'll take that over the alternatives. As far as I'm concerned, it's better—and healthier—to laugh than overeat. (Laughing also burns calories. How convenient!) These are tough times for all of us. If you don't believe me, turn on the TV, read a newspaper, or just listen to me argue politics with my father.

But there's hope that life will work out. I found hope, and continue to find it, in unlikely places. And I've seen other people find it, too. We have a new president who, agree with him or not, recognizes that hope above all else is what offers light on the darkest of days.

I came to realize (and I hope you will, too) that success isn't measured solely by stepping on the scale. That's part of it. But the way you and I want to feel goes beyond what we weigh every morning. You have to pay attention to the voice you hear in your head (the good one) and the feeling in your heart.

As you read further, you will see that I have tried to tell the kinds of stories that I would have wanted to hear or needed to hear as I switched gears from dieting to maintenance. In a way, it's as if I'm opening up my underwear drawer for the world to look at. You're going to find all styles and colors—except for granny panties—and learn about the stuff that wasn't necessarily visible, the stuff that happened to me on the inside as I continued on this crazy, fun, frustrating, emotional, and joyous journey of trying to create my best and healthiest self.

Two years ago I set out to lose weight. I succeeded, but ended up embarking on a whole other journey to find whatever that elusive thing was that had been missing in my life; the thing that once I found it, would give me peace and make me feel good, as if everything was okay and as it should be; the thing that would satisfy my physical as well as inner hunger.

This is my story of that search.

One more thing: please know that I don't always know what I'm doing, but I know that trying is much better than the alternative. If life has one constant, it's change. Like it or not, all of us experience change. We change diapers, change outfits, change relationships, jobs, dress sizes, ages, opinions . . . or change the way we look at ourselves and, ultimately, our lives.

I needed to make a change in my life, a big one, and I did. In order to maintain that success, I realized I needed, and in fact wanted, to continue to transform and evolve. And along the way I realized that the constant remolding of our gooey center is the key to enjoying life's desserts—even if we are watching our weight.

Part One

Faith

Chapter One

The Sex Talk

The only time I enjoyed being fat was when I was pregnant. I weighed nearly 180 pounds, and I was in heaven. As I ate Italian subs that my mom made to tide me over between meals, I would smile at the thought of the miracle of bringing a life into this world, a life that I would raise and nurture, guide and fill with love and wisdom. It was a special time in my life.

I did not think the same thing when that miraculous creation of mine called on the phone from the road where he was touring with his father's band and said, "Hey, Ma, can I sleep at my girlfriend's house?"

I wanted to vomit.

Actually, I wanted to open the fridge and eat everything on the second shelf, the third shelf, and then the top shelf. Not even the old brick of cheddar with the mold on it was safe from the surge of anxiety and uncertainty I felt at that moment.

I kept my head on, though, and said, "I don't think it's a good idea."

After we'd said goodbye, I held the phone at arm's length in shock. Wolfie's question lingered in the air, like a smoke signal in an old western portending imminent danger.

I looked around for Tom to ask him how I had gotten to this place. He had gone outside, which was lucky for me. With gleeful sarcasm, he would have reminded me that this situation was the result of one night nearly eighteen years earlier when I had gotten frisky with my then-husband, Ed. Now I had a sixteen-and-three-quarters-year-old teenager who wanted to sleep with his girl-friend.

Then Tom came through the front door whistling his happy tune. I was still debating whether to eat or throw up. I filled him in on the news.

"Tell me again—what did Wolfie say exactly?" he asked.

"He said he wanted to sleep at Liv's house," I said.

"Well, that's not exactly saying he wants to sleep *with* her," he said.

"You're talking semantics," I said. "I'm thinking sex."

"You are?" he said, his face unfolding in a giant smile.

"Oh, shut up," I snapped. "What is it with men? I'm in a quandary, and you've somehow turned this around and think you're going to get lucky."

"I'm not?" he asked, with a sad face.

"Come on," I said. "Help me think this through."

We sat down at the kitchen table and talked. Tom pointed out that Wolfie had called home to ask permission. He hadn't slept over at Liv's house, even though he was halfway across the country and traveling as part of a rock-and-roll band. Tom suggested I think about how Wolfie's dad had been at that same age, something that made me say a quick prayer of thanks. Wolfie knew right from wrong, Tom pointed out. If he didn't, he was trying to figure it out and had looked to his mother for advice. He was a good kid. *Ergo*, what was I worried about?

"Losing him!" I said with an exaggerated whimper.

At the time, I weighed 132.2 pounds, down 40 pounds from when I had begun a very public diet earlier that spring. I had already surpassed my original weight loss goal of 30 pounds and at some point—I had failed to note it on my calendar—I had gone from losing weight to being on maintenance.

I had talked about maintenance for months as if it were a change of life. But I had no idea what it was really about. I figured I would learn once I got there. Then I got there and wondered what it was that I was supposed to be maintaining. My life was in flux—it wasn't a work-in-progress as much as it was simply work. As I would find out, maintenance was exactly that—more work. And it was life work, not losing-weight work.

If my weight was a barometer of the rest of my life, I still wasn't where I wanted to be. In addition to concern about my weight, I also knew that I could be better, kinder, smarter, more disciplined, compassionate, patient, and loving. I wanted to feel like I mattered. I yearned for a lightness of being that couldn't be measured on a scale. I wanted to feel whole, peaceful, and connected to a Higher Power even if just for a few moments.

But real life made that seem impossible. Whether it was Wolfie being away from home, Tom's struggles to be a hands-on father to his children, my career, the house falling apart, or my anger at Bush and Cheney for where they had taken the country, I was unable to relax much less get a firm grip. Then Wolfie fell in love and I felt as if part of the floor had given way.

"What about condoms?" Tom mused one day.

"What do you mean by that?" I asked.

"For Wolfie," he said.

I looked at him, aghast at his insensitivity.

"Not funny."

I liked Wolfie's girlfriend, Liv, who was a friend of Tom's oldest daughter. Wolfie had met her the previous summer in Arizona, but he never appeared to take any special interest in her. Nor did she in him. One time he mentioned that she bugged him. I should have taken note.

Then Liv and her family moved to Kansas and we didn't hear about her. In the meantime, Wolfie went on tour. We talked every couple of days. He was semi-good about keeping in touch. He texted me from Indianapolis and phoned from Chicago and Detroit. He had a story about each city. Then he called from Kansas, where in an unusually excited voice, he said that he had the day off and that he and Matt, the young man who drove his tour bus and watched out for him, had been invited to eat dinner at Liv's house. He asked if I remembered Liv. Had I developed Alzheimer's since he'd gone out on tour with Van Halen a few months earlier? Of course, I remembered her. He said that Liv's mom had invited them to have a home-cooked meal.

"Isn't that nice of them?" he said.

"Yes, it is," I said.

"I'm so excited," he said.

Wolfie was never that effusive unless he saw a new gadget at the Apple store. All of a sudden I paid more attention. My son hadn't sounded like himself when he had asked, "Is that nice of them?" He crossed the line when he said, "I'm so excited." I realized he was telling me that there was more to this invitation than dinner. He liked this girl.

It was one of those subtle moments in life when you open your eyes and discover that the pieces that have provided longtime familiarity in a relationship have shifted slightly in one direction or another. It's like waking up in the morning and remembering that you rearranged a couple pieces of furniture in the room. You have to create new walkways so you don't bump into things.

I'm not someone who likes change. I have had the furniture in my living room for twenty years. I bought it with Ed early in our marriage. I have been meaning to get it recovered for the past five years. It shows you how fast I move. I wasn't ready for my son to have a girlfriend and everything that meant. Is any mother ever ready to relinquish her place as first in their child's heart? I wasn't.

I told Tom, who digested the news with a calm nod. It made me suspicious. I asked if he had known that anything was going on between Wolfie and *his daughter's friend*, Liv. I emphasized Liv's relationship to Andie not to remind him of who this girl was but to instead put him on notice that everything that happened between them from here on out was his fault. He understood and shook his head no.

"You can't do that to me," he said.

"Yes I can," I said.

"I'll find out what's going on," he said.

"Good idea," I said.

Like a dutiful soldier in the age-old battle of parents vs. children, Tom reported back that Wolfie was indeed tight with Liv. I felt a little like an editor at a tabloid magazine. But so what. I wanted to know everything Tom had found out. According to his source, they had been texting and talking on the telephone for months. Wolfie had fallen into "deep like" with this pretty girl, and from the information Tom had turned up, she felt the same way about him.

"So it's all good," Tom said,

"All good?" I asked.

"I wonder if they've kissed," he said, ignoring me.

"Stop!"

"What do you mean?" he asked.

"I don't want to know if they've kissed or anything else," I said.

"You don't?" he asked. "Now's the time when you want to know everything. Well, not everything. But you want to know what's going on."

"I hate it when you're right."

Late that afternoon, Wolfie phoned home and reported on dinner at Liv's. His voice was upbeat and I could hear that he was happy, very happy. Wolfie's willingness to talk was a surefire indicator of his moods. When his voice was soft and he used words as sparingly as a nomad would drink water in the desert, I knew there was trouble. Now I couldn't shut him up. He told me everything Liv's mother had served for dinner and every bit of conversation at the table.

It was a little overboard even for him. I wanted to ask, are you really my kid?

"And guess what?" he asked.

"What?"

"They invited me to sleep over after dinner. Can I?"

"I don't think it's a good idea," I said.

"But Ma!"

"Wolfie, it's very nice of Liv and her family to want you to sleep at their house. But you have a hotel room and a show the next day. I'm sure Dad's going to want you there."

Grudgingly, he agreed. I was sure his willingness to listen to me stemmed from the newness of this relationship and the other circumstances of his living situation. I reminded myself that he had called to ask my permission rather than decide on his own, which was the way I had tried to raise him. When you don't know something, ask someone for advice, preferably your parent—and that's just what he'd done. But I wondered how long he would continue to listen to me. I was a year younger than he was when I got involved in my first serious romance and I worked myself into a full steam of anxiety remembering what I had done and not told my parents.

If it had been possible, I might have flown to Kansas and brought Wolfie back home for the night. I had the urge to have my little boy back, the one who used to look at me with blind devotion and raise his arms high in the air and say, "Mama up!" I didn't want to think about him having a girlfriend and all the complications that might ensure. But as Tom reminded me when he got home, this wasn't about me. Even though I wasn't ready for him to have a girlfriend, he was and I would have to deal with it.

"I supposed that's why God invented M&Ms and potato chips," I said, jokingly.

"No," Tom laughed. "But I think it's why He invented the phone, the video camera, iChat, private detectives, and so on."

Luckily for me, within a few days, Tom and I visited Wolfie on tour. The trip had been planned months earlier, so it didn't seem like I was checking up on him. Though delighted to see us, Wolfie still needed a little time to adjust to having his mom out there with him. I understood. I upset the routine he got into of studying during the day, going to soundcheck, performing, eating dinner late, and then staying up even later as he wound down from the show. It wasn't exactly the day of a normal sixteen-year-old. But that's the reason I visited as frequently as I did. I thought whatever facsimile of family time I could manufacture would be better than none.

On this trip, though, I had questions. I asked the obvious mom-type questions before the show. I didn't ask about Liv until the show was finished and we were back at the hotel, playing cards in the two-bedroom suite Wolfie shared with Matt. Wolfie was much more relaxed than he had been prior to the show, which I reminded myself made sense considering he had many things on his mind before performing onstage in front of twenty thousand people. Finally, I asked how dinner at Liv's had been. All of a sudden he perked up. His eyes opened wide and he began to recount the dinner in the same detail as he had on the phone. Except this time, in the course of telling me the story, he mentioned that he liked Liv.

"Oh, really?" I said, drawing on thirty-six years of acting experience to deliver that note of nonchalant curiosity.

"Yeah," he said. "The way I felt about her last summer . . ."

"You liked her last summer?" I interrupted.

"Now it's not the same, you know?"

"Good for you," I said. "She's a very nice girl."

"Really nice," he said.

We spent Thanksgiving with my parents and brother, Pat, and his wife, Stacy, in Arizona. Wolfie was there with us, regaling everyone with stories from the road and catching up with Tom's son, Tony, and friends. After the holiday, Liv flew in and stayed with us for a week. I was more nervous than she appeared to be; in fact, I had to remind myself that I was the parent, not the girlfriend visiting the boyfriend's family. The problem was, I didn't know how to play my role, whether to be strict or cool or super cool or what.

Pretty quickly I figured out that I really liked Liv, who impressed me as a mature and together young woman. I could tell that she had been raised properly. She was considerate and well-mannered. When she arrived, I had her put her suitcase in Wolfie and Tony's room and made it clear the two boys would sleep in the plush tour bus parked in front of the house. She thanked me for allowing her to visit.

Very late that night, I woke up in a panic, wondering where Wolfie and Liv were sleeping. They had not given me a single reason to suspect they weren't in the places I had assigned them earlier in the day, but my mind was full of scenarios that filled me with concern. It was because I had been a teenager once, and I knew what I had done at that same age. Actually, I'd been younger. Was that beside the point? Or was it the point? I had no idea. Nor did it matter. I got out of bed and crept through the house like a guard on the show *Lockup*. As I tiptoed back into the bedroom and quietly slipped back under the covers, Tom rolled over.

"And?" he asked.

"Everyone's where they're supposed to be," I said.

"Except for you."

"Touché," I replied.

I shut my eyes and tried to go back to sleep while realizing something that many parents before me had discovered: I was the one with sex on the brain, not Wolfie or Liv. I knew that would change if they stayed together, but for now this was more my issue than theirs. I supposed it was part of being a parent. I had the wisdom and experience to know what lay ahead, and to prepare for it.

Was I prepared? I didn't know; I'd have to see when I got there, wherever that would be.

There was a more important question: Was Wolfie prepared? Had I done my job as a parent?

I thought about two things: The talks I hadn't had with him about sex and love and maturity, and the discussions I should have had with him about relationships, the highs, lows, joys, difficulties, and potential of heartbreak. We had spent hours discussing favorite movies such as *Galaxy Quest* and *Lord of the Rings*. We had also talked endlessly about the video game *Legend of Zelda*. We had discussed school, music, favorite bands, clothes, acne, friends—all the stuff that happened. I had at times even solicited his opinion on stuff I had seen in the Pottery Barn catalog? How had I managed to not talk to him about girls, sex, and love? What was wrong with me?

I felt like a bad mother. I worried that I had failed both of us.

I still felt that way in the morning. As I made myself coffee, I thought about handling those feelings in the way I had done so many times in the past: by opening the fridge and eating my way into numbness. I didn't do it. I knew it wasn't a healthy or productive way to handle a problem. I had learned that I was an emotional eater, and as such, I had come to recognize my desire to eat during times of upset or stress for what it was—an emotional response to a feeling that is starved for action or discussion, not a desire for a slice of leftover pizza at 9:30 in the morning.

I heard Tom stirring and took him a cup of coffee. I asked if he wanted to go for a walk, explaining that I needed to work off something that was bothering me.

"What's up?" he asked.

"I haven't had the sex talk," I said.

He put his hands on my shoulders, pulled me close and said, "Baby, we don't have to talk about it."

I pushed him away.

"Not you, silly," I said. "I haven't talked to Wolfie about sex."

"Doesn't he know where babies come from?"

"I'm sure he does. It's how they're made that I'm not sure he understands completely."

"Or how to keep them from being made."

"Thank you."

"I'm sure he knows that part, too."

"But I'm not sure," I said.

"It's a little late, don't you think?" Tom said. "Besides, he's probably seen everything and then some in the movies or on the Internet."

"Yeah, but I know seeing it and talking about it are two different things." I took a deep breath and sighed. "This isn't fair."

"What isn't?"

"Wolfie's still in bed, sleeping soundly without a care in his head other than what he and Liv are going to do today—and I'm pacing the kitchen, wondering if dipping Cheetoes in peanut butter might make me feel better about not ever having talked to my son about sex."

"Probably not," Tom said. "I think we should take a walk."

"Yeah, good idea."

I had a good, albeit sardonic laugh as I thought of being on maintenance in the context of my life. First, let me say that I wasn't yet on maintenance. I was looking ahead. In reality, thanks to a handful of macaroons, I was up one third of a pound, which meant I still had a pound and a half to go before I reached my weight loss goal. On my blog, I wrote, "Guys, what if I'm on maintenance next week?"

What if I was?

That's what made me laugh.

What was I trying to maintain beyond my weight—and even that wasn't set in stone?

I made a list in my head, and the things I needed to fix or change outnumbered the things I was content to merely maintain.

Who came up with this concept of maintenance?

I realized my life was similar to my closet. No matter what time or year, it could always use a little straightening or cleaning. The job was never finished. Motherhood was the same. The problems changed, but they didn't end or get any easier. At one point when Tom and I were on our walk, I looked up at the sky and mused, "Oh really, God. Why didn't you tell me that it wasn't going to ever end or get easier—or that the poopy diapers were just a warm-up?"

The following afternoon, I had an opportunity to talk with Wolfie. I found him on the sofa, watching TV. Alone! Miraculously, he wasn't with Liv. The two of them spent more time together than co-joined twins. I seized the moment.

"Hey, I want to talk about you and Liv," I said, trying to sound casual and relaxed as I plopped down on the sofa.

"Yeah, Mom. What's up?"

"We've never officially or even unofficially talked about sex," I said. "You know, the sex talk."

"You mean where babies come from?" he asked.

"No, more like how babies are made."

"Ma!"

"What?"

"Please don't go there," he said.

"Really?"

"It's gross."

"But you're in a relationship."

"It's gross."

I took a deep breath. I agreed with him. I was uncomfortable and embarrassed talking about sex with my son, not that I would characterize what we were doing as talking about sex. But I wanted to make a point. Unfortunately for me, I hadn't thought that part through to a conclusive place I could articulate. In my head, I had only gotten as far as "we need to talk."

So I just looked at Wolfie until he said, "What? What are you looking at?" How could I explain what I was looking at? I was looking at sixteen years of life, his remarkable growth, my frustrating inadequacies, and the fact that in the beginning it had been just the two of us and now here we were, the two of us brought together yet again by the miracle of life. I could have, and probably should have, just been forthright and said that from the little intelligence I had been able to gather, I knew that he and Liv were still as chaste as the Jonas Brothers, and I wanted to keep it that way, at least for a while. But if things were to change, here's what I wanted him to know. Here's what I had learned about men and women, sex and responsibility. But there wasn't a chance in hell of that coming out of my mouth.

I also thought about asking if he would take a vow of chastity and I would take a vow of silence and the two of us would meet back here in a few years. But that didn't happen either. Instead, I blurted out that I was looking forward to being a grandmother

someday. But he was way too young to start giving me grandchil-
dren.

Wolfie responded exactly as I would have if I had been sixteen
and sitting cross from me after that ridiculous statement. He stared
at me with a look of startled bewilderment. I shrugged. I thought
it was a nice try—the best I could do.

"Do you feel better now?" he asked.

"I don't know," I said.

"Mom, let me just talk to Dad about it," he said. "How about
that?"

"Fine."

Relieved, I walked out of the room. About two minutes later, I
was kicked in the butt by reality. I couldn't believe what I had
agreed to. Had I lost my mind? God only knew what kind of information Wolfie might get from his dad. Getting your sex talk from
Eddie Van Halen wasn't recommended in any of the parenting
books I read.

A few days later, Liv flew back home, Wolfie went back on the
road, and I reached my goal of losing 40 pounds. I celebrated the
milestone at the kitchen table in my sweats, asking myself what
now? Maintenance? Ha! Instead of throwing myself a party for
hitting my goal, as I had always expected to do, I went for a hike
with Tom up and down Pinnacle Peak, a rugged mountain outside
of Phoenix.

As we huffed and puffed, I asked Tom if his parents had ever
talked to him about sex. They hadn't, he said. He had learned
about the facts of life from friends on the playground. I had discovered that information the same way, separating fact from fiction
as I went along. Did anyone get the formal, sit-down sex talk? Or

was that just a chapter in the parenting books that everyone skipped?

"I'd like to think that I progressed beyond my parents," I said.

"Well, I have always spoken pretty openly about sex to my girls," Tom said. "They even told me when they got their periods."

"Aren't you evolved," I said.

He grinned.

"I just recently told your mother that I've seen your penis," I said.

"What?" he said. "What'd she say?"

" 'Oh, honey. I've seen it too. It's no big thing!' " I said, laughing.

By the time we returned home, I had put all joking aside and decided to speak to my son again and make sure we had the kind of talk that I knew in my heart was right. I wanted to make sure he was prepared, responsible and sensitive—and informed—if only for my own peace of mind or just to prove that I could do better than my parents. I knew that I would beat myself up if I didn't do it.

Later that day, after working up my determination and thinking about what I wanted to say, I called Wolfie at his hotel. He was waiting for Matt to finish bundling gear before they headed to the arena.

"Do you remember the talk I wanted to have with you after Thanksgiving?" I said.

"Maybe," he said.

"The one about sex," I said.

"Ma!"

"Have you spoken with your dad about it yet?"

"No."

"Good," I said. "I wanted to get to you first."

"Ma, it's gross—and whatever happens between me and Liv, it's none of your business."

"You're right," I said. "That would be gross, as you say. I don't want to know about the two of you. This isn't about Liv, in fact. It's about you." I paused momentarily, waiting for him to cut me off. He didn't—and I knew right then I had him and this was my time.

"Look, I just want to tell you that as far as you and Liv or you and anyone else that comes into your life goes, it's about your heart and hers. Don't give your heart and self away easily. But when you do, don't protect it to the point where you don't open yourself up to your feelings. Always be kind and treat other people the way you want to be—"

"Ma, I know," he said, cutting me off. "Treat people the way I want to be treated. You say it all the time. I get it."

"One more thing," I said.

"What?"

"Babies come from storks."

Relieved, I told Tom about the conversation. I don't know if it was helpful, but I felt better.

A few days later, all of us rendezvoused at the Van Halen concert in San Diego. Before the show, I pulled Ed aside and asked him to speak to Wolfie about being responsible and sensitive in relationships. I didn't come right out and say he was serious about his girlfriend and we needed to make sure he was well informed. But Ed understood. I saw him take it in, think about what he should say, and then he looked at his girlfriend Janie, at me, and at Tom, and nodded.

"Got it," he said.

I was nervous about what he might say, because he could be

crude even when trying to be sensitive. But I felt like I had run out of options. God help me, I turned it over to Ed.

A little before the show, I was standing with Tom in the hallway outside Ed's dressing room when I thought I overheard him having *the talk*. I shushed Tom and inched closer to the doorway. Tom was right behind me when I turned around and we heard Ed tell Wolfie to listen to his heart, to be careful of who he gave it to, and then "when you give it away be careful of their heart, too." Then he added, "Treat each other with kindness."

I gritted my teeth at Tom.

"That's what I tried to tell him," I said.

"Shush," Tom said. "They're still going."

We listened closer and heard Ed finish: ". . . and be wary of all the sluts and skanks and whores who will want to be with you because you play in a band and have a famous last name."

I shrugged. I wouldn't have said that last part. But it was essentially the same talk I had tried to have. I wanted to praise Ed, but remembered that we were eavesdropping and quickly grabbed Tom and guided us away from the door. Then Wolfie strolled out and into the hall. He was in a good mood.

"Hey, Ma," he said.

"What's going on?" I asked.

"Nothing," he said. "Just talking to Dad."

I watched him walk back to his dressing room. All of us were learning about the facts of life.

Notes to Myself

Drink more water! Thirst is different from hunger. Thirst for knowledge, thirst for health, thirst for love . . . lots of water.

Today, my mind and body are in conflict about going to the gym, but I'm telling them to get on the same page! How? I'm thinking of all the times I've wished I'd worked out but couldn't. And the times I've wished I'd felt good about myself but didn't. Now that I have the time to get exercise . . . is forty-five minutes such a big deal?

Tom says I snore. He doesn't. We're an odd couple.

Chapter Two

The Driver's Test

What do you do for an encore after you've changed your life?

I asked myself that question as we sped across the Mojave Desert. It was New Year's Eve, and Tom, Wolfie, Tom's son Tony, and I were driving to Los Angeles from Scottsdale. I had asked everyone to share their resolutions.

"Guys, if you don't say anything, I'm going to make them for you," I said.

They looked like I had asked one of them to walk the rest of the way. Just blank faces and dumb stares.

"It's not like you're being recorded," I said. "Just say something."

"V, what about you?" Tony asked.

I got all set to speak, and then I drew a blank, too. I couldn't think of anything to say. I'm not big on New Year's Eve celebrations and am usually ho-hum about making resolutions. They just invite disappointment. Besides, I had already made more than my share of resolutions the previous forty-seven years, and I didn't want to seem like I was hogging all the good ones.

I made a feeble attempt at getting out of the jam by joking that I was on maintenance, and my goal was to keep everything status quo. That earned me a chorus of boos from the peanut gallery. So I made resolutions for other people. I said I wanted politicians to have clarity. I wanted the parents and families of soldiers fighting in the Middle East to see their loved ones return home safely. I wanted health for my parents and success and happiness for Tom and his children.

"I'd love to see peace . . ."

"Oh, no, there she goes again, getting all Gandhi on us," Wolfie interrupted. "Come on, Mom. What about you?"

"I told you," I said. "I'm not making any."

"Mom!"

Because we had three-and-a-half more hours together in the car, I acquiesced. I thought about the notes I made to myself, the endless To Do lists I made. I said I wanted to finally hire a contractor to draw up plans so we could start renovating the house before the backyard deck slid down the hillside. I also said that I wanted to drink more water, which was met by shouts of "weak!" I felt like I couldn't win.

"Okay," I finally said. "I want to improve as a person."

He rolled his eyes. But I was being pragmatic. Losing weight had been like an amazing reveal after a magic trick, a big ta-da. After years of using food to keep myself from facing the fears and insecurity of my life, I had come out of hiding. I had woken up and started becoming the person I had always wanted to be. I no longer looked in the mirror and disliked the woman I saw. Nor did I walk around with a frown, avoiding eye contact and wishing I were invisible. I was beginning to really like this new me—and even on days when I didn't, I was still pretty darn happy.

However, I knew that I was not yet a finished product. Not even close. Off camera and in the privacy of my real life, I was raw, vulnerable, curious, and uncertain. Although I had put some problems behind me, I faced new challenges. Now that I felt better about being me, I wanted more—more confidence, more experiences, more insights, and understanding. I was frustrated that I couldn't think of any resolutions, because I felt as if I had a long list of them.

I didn't know how to articulate it—this new kind of hunger. It was like when you eat something delicious and don't want it to end. I had felt that same way after dieting and exercising for the last nine months—I wasn't ready to stop. But I didn't know what to do next other than doing more of the same. I needed a plan, or at least to see where I was supposed to be headed.

Tom has always had a deep belief in God, and I was intrigued by the sense of calm he seemed to get whenever he "let go and let God." For many reasons, chief among them that I was haunted by the irrational concern that too many good things were happening to me so something terrible must be ahead, I could have used a dose of letting go and letting God. I made a mental note of adding that to my To Do list.

"I know a resolution you could make," Wolfie said.

"Let me hear it," I said reluctantly.

"You could try to be more patient when I'm driving," he said. "It would be great if you didn't scream 'hit the brake' all the time."

• • •

With that, Wolfie opened a Pandora's Box that we continued to deal with long into the new year. At sixteen and three-quarters years old, Wolfie could already have had his driver's license. But he didn't. A year earlier, when he had been eligible to get his learner's permit, we had made a plan that both Wolfie and Tony would go through the process at the same time. They took the practice tests online in their bedroom.

It seemed like an invitation to cheat. But they clearly didn't. Tony came out smiling, followed by Wolfie, who looked bummed. Depressed at failing the test, he moped around until he was able to take it again. When he passed, his self-confidence bounced back. He would need that resiliency, of course, once he got behind the wheel.

Although Tom and Ed drove with him, I bore the primary responsibility of taking Wolfie out for practice drives. I was mostly okay with that since I considered myself a better driver than either of them. (Of course, both men would disagree with me. Imagine that!) I swore I wouldn't be the kind of parent who sat in the passenger seat, barking orders to turn, stop, and watch out. The first time we got in the car, I promised Wolfie that I would be cool.

"Just remember to buckle up," I said.

"Ma!"

"And turn the ignition key gently."

"Mom, I've started a car before," he said.

"Sorry. I'll keep quiet."

But months later, I was still shouting instructions at him when we got in the car. I wasn't as bad as I had been when I was in labor and swearing at Ed, but I came close. Even when there wasn't any traffic nearby, I warned Wolfie to watch out, check his mirrors, and drive defensively. It was as though I had some disorder and it got more severe in proportion to the number of other cars on the road.

Finally, one day he pulled over to the side of the road and said, "Mom, stop it!"

"What am I doing?"

"You're making me nervous," he said. "*You* are going to cause an accident."

Not only was he right, he woke me up to my behavior. I hadn't been aware that I was the source of most of his nervousness behind the wheel. It explained why everyone from Tom to my brother, Patrick, and his wife, Stacy, in Arizona, all of whom had driven with Wolfie, reported that he was a good driver. Everyone saw it except me. I had to ask myself why I was so critical of him when he was driving. Ordinarily, I was Wolfie's biggest cheerleader. What changed once we got in the car?

After some time, I figured it out. When I got in the car with him, I lacked one of life's essential ingredients: faith. You can tick off the top five necessities of life, and faith has to be included among chocolate, pasta, and butter. (As for the fifth, love? A warm bed? Salt? I'll leave it open to debate.) Anyway, Wolfie had been driving long enough for me to see that my fear and apprehension was unwarranted, at least to the degree that I shouted instructions at him. Why didn't I have more faith in him?

I'd had blind faith in so many other endeavors, ranging from the first time I walked out in front of a live audience on the set of *One Day at a Time*, to marrying Ed when I was twenty, to having a baby ten years later. As I thought about it, bringing another life into the world was the ultimate exercise in faith. I don't know what had made me think I could raise a child, but I did.

I'd also had faith in myself when I finally split with Ed. Although it had taken twenty years, once I made the decision to do it, I was determined to land on my feet. It didn't turn out to be as simple as walking onstage or having a baby. In the aftermath of divorce, though, I made two crucial leaps of faith. I opened my heart to Tom, and I decided that I'd had enough of being depressed and self-defeating, which, it turned out, was the step I'd needed to say yes to Jenny Craig.

How did I know that would work? I didn't. I had faith—just as I continued to have faith that I would keep the weight off.

My problem with Wolfie's driving was largely an emotional issue. Rationally, I knew he was a capable young man. He was my go-to guy for computer help. He performed in front of an arena full of people with total professionalism. If anyone had questioned his sense of responsibility, I would have been his loudest and strongest defender. I would have even defended him as a driver.

But I freaked out when I thought about him getting behind the wheel of a car and driving away on his own. Other than his lack of experience, which applied to everyone his age, I knew my fear was mostly irrational. I told myself that I needed to let go for both our sakes. I needed to have faith he would get where he needed to go and return home safely.

At the time, faith was something on my mind, particularly in a political sense. As a news junkie, I knew from reports that President Bush's approval rating had dropped to an all-time low of 27 percent and then had slightly risen in January to 33 percent. By contrast, six years earlier, he had enjoyed a nearly 90 percent approval rating. I knew that meant that much of the country had lost faith in the president.

By both contrast and necessity, we were looking elsewhere for a new leader. The presidential election was only ten months away. I was thinking long and hard about which of the candidates would provide me with faith that they could take America in a new and better direction. I watched Oprah Winfrey help launch Barack Obama's campaign in Iowa and then followed his stops in South Carolina and New Hampshire. I was inspired by his energy and charisma, his ability as speaker and his plans to fix the country's problems.

I loved that he was younger and smarter than me, and I would love it even more later on as he emerged as the Democrats' choice. It spoke volumes to me about hope for the country's future.

At the time, though, Hillary Clinton was still my choice. I liked her experience, I thought she was brilliant and liked that she was a woman.

I could get behind either Obama or Clinton. I thought either could do a better job than the man who had held the job for the previous eight years. I looked forward to the change of administration and not getting worked up every time I saw either Bush or Cheney on television putting forth some argument or policy I didn't agree with or trust.

I felt like Bush's parting gift was the optimism he was giving to Democrats like me after eight years of misery. It buoyed my outlook, and that optimism rubbed off on other things, including my attitude toward Wolfie's driving. If I could survive the Bush administration, I could also make it through my son's days as a student driver.

One day, I got in the car with him and decided to make an effort to think positively. I watched as he checked his mirrors before pulling out. I noticed that he came to a complete stop at the Stop sign at the bottom of our hill, something I more than a few times had failed to do myself. Finally I saw the way he parked effortlessly in the grocery store's crowded lot. Hey, what was I worried about?

"Nice job," I said.

"Really?" he replied, his face brightening with pleasure. "Cool."

Wolfie and I put together a string of successful trips. We would get home afterward, and Tom and Tony would look at us expectantly for clues about how we had treated each other. I would say he did great. Then Wolfie and Tony would go off by themselves to jam, and Tom would ask me how our trip had *really* gone. I would tell him that I genuinely believed that I had improved as a passenger.

"What about Wolfie?"

"He was fine."

Tom and I had wanted to take Wolfie and Tony to the DMV to get their licenses at the same time. Unfortunately for Tony, who was eager to get his license, Wolfie wasn't in a hurry. He was born two weeks late and has done things on his own timetable ever since. Being on the road where he traveled by private jet, tour bus, and limousine made getting his license a low priority until he returned home and wanted to visit friends.

Once he was back, I made an appointment at the DMV and took both boys for their temporary licenses. They walked in with their driver's manuals and leafed through them while waiting in line for their eye exams, which both passed. Then they took their written tests in another room. I waited nervously, thinking I would read the book I had brought but in reality just fidgeting and worrying.

About thirty minutes later, the boys emerged and handed their tests back for grading. Tony's was first, and he passed, but Wolfie missed too many answers and failed. He didn't want to talk about it.

"Mom, I know you're going to try to make me feel better," he said. "But you can't, so don't even try."

"Not even a little bit?" I said.

"No."

Six weeks later, he failed the written test again. He had studied the manual more than the last time but obviously not enough. Figuring the notion that misery loves company, I told him about other kids who had failed the test multiple times despite studying. I even mentioned a few adults who'd had trouble. He didn't care. He got down on himself and wasn't interested in further talk about scheduling a third attempt.

Seeing him avoid the subject and make half-hearted, self-deprecating jokes about his failure to pass reminded me of the worst of myself. I didn't want him repeating my mistakes; I wanted to break him out of that cycle. One day, we were in the car and, again figuring that misery likes company, I considered telling him about some of my failures. But he knew those as well as I did.

He didn't want to talk about it anyway, and he especially didn't want to hear my opinion on what he needed to do to pass the test. Then he went back on the road, which allowed him to forget about the test for a while. Not me. I continued to think about my son and this minor hurdle he had to get over.

"He just needs to study the manual," Tony said.

His advice was as obvious as the fact that the person who needed to hear those words was in a hotel room somewhere halfway across the country, not in the kitchen where Tony was grabbing lunch before heading to work. I left it to him to pass that information on to Wolfie, which he said he had hinted at and would do again. After he left, Tom and I headed out for a hike in a nearby canyon.

I had learned to like exercising when I felt stressed and emotional. I couldn't say trudging up the large hill Tom and I were on beat the short-term satisfaction of burying my face in a bag of chips, but it was healthier. I got a sense of being in control of my feelings and able to cope.

"I still hate this damn hill," I said.

"We have to bear trials as a test," Tom said.

"A test of what?" I asked.

"Our faith," he said.

"You're quoting Bible verses now?"

"It's the first chapter of James. It's gotten people through difficult circumstances for thousands of years," he said.

"Like this damn hill?" I asked.

"Much bigger."

We quit talking and focused on the walk. I enjoyed this part of the hike, when my arms pumped in synch with my breathing and I felt into the rhythm of my body exerting itself. It felt good, and I didn't think of anything else until we stopped for a quick rest and water break at a bench near the top of the hill.

I thought back to the first time we had done this hike. I barely had made it to the bench before falling to my knees and complaining I couldn't go any farther. But then I got up and went a little bit more. Now that I was lighter, I felt stronger and fitter. I felt like I could do almost anything—short of helping my kid pass the written part of his driver's license test. I guessed that this was his lesson to learn.

On his next break from the tour, Wolfie came home and wanted to take the test again. It turned out Tony had talked to him about studying the book and, as he later said, Wolfie had practically memorized the manual and there was no way he was not going to pass it this third time. I didn't end up going to the DMV. As it happened, Tom needed to renew his license and he took Wolfie. When they returned home a few hours later, Wolfie was waving his test like the American flag at the head of a Fourth of July parade. He had passed.

I gave him a hug that nearly broke his ribs and said, "Thank you, Lord."

"Don't thank Him," Tom said. "Wolfie passed because he finally decided to crack the book."

"I heard that," Wolfie said.

"And?" I asked.

"Well, I guess it's true," he shrugged.

With the written test behind him, Tom took Wolfie back to the DMV to get his actual driver's license. Even though all of us agreed the hard part was over, Wolfie asked me to stay home, explaining that I made him nervous. I was mildly hurt, but at the same time I was a little relieved. I waved goodbye, wished them luck, and made Tom promise to call as soon as there was news.

More than an hour went by without a call from either one of them. I tried calling them, but neither picked up. Wolfie'd had an appointment. They should have already been done. Not knowing drove me crazy. I was standing outside by the front door when they finally drove up. Wolfie was in the driver's seat with a smile on his face as wide as the windshield, so I knew he had passed.

I looked up at the sky and saw a string of puffy white clouds lined up like chariots. It was a beautiful day.

Notes to Myself

❧

Instead of trying to do everything today, pick one realistic goal and do that.

What are realistic goals? Honesty, being on time, returning calls and e-mails . . . things that relieve stress . . . and making sure all the bathrooms are stocked with toilet paper.

Remember, you are not trying to lose weight or maintain the weight you've lost so much as you're trying to continue to improve the way you think about your body and therefore yourself, since you *are* your body. Make *that* connection.

"Do not wish to be anything but what you are, and try to be that perfectly."—St. Francis de Sales.

Oh, really, Francis? You're a saint.

Chapter Three

Getting Naked

After my first book, *Losing It*, was published, I was asked intensely personal questions about my marriage, past romances, and drug use. I was mostly questioned about my diet and how I'd achieved my recent weight loss, though people seemed to be equally fascinated with the fact that I *had* gotten fat, as in, How could you have let yourself get that big?

I knew what I was getting into when I wrote the book, so I had no problem with the questions, whether they were about dating Steven Spielberg, life with my ex-husband, or experimenting with drugs. Even though I was best known for playing other people, I was unexpectedly comfortable in this new role as myself. I didn't really care who knew what about me.

What was there to hide? I'd already told the world I was fat. Now my life was literally an open book. Oprah homed in on the last and only real intimate secret I had left when she asked about my memoir's revelation that I had once kissed another woman. It was no big deal. As I learned while doing book signings, for most people, my life's more prurient moments aren't as interesting as my history as a reformed fatty. They mostly wanted to hear about my trek through the Valley of the Shadow of Overweightness.

Although happy to comply, I was surprised and unprepared for the pressure of being held up as an inspiration for change. It was one thing for Obama to stand in front of a banner that said "Change You Can Believe In." It was another for me to do the same. Yes, I had lost weight. I looked different, and better. But was the change real? Would it be long-lasting? Would it be permanent?

Privately, I had trouble believing it was real, even though I'd vowed to keep this new me. I worried I might be a big fat fraud hiding in a thin-person's suit. I worried that I might let down any-one and everyone who saw me as an inspiration. After all, I hadn't cured cancer. I had just lost 40 pounds and was living my life. I didn't understand that these feelings of doubt were normal, part of having good and bad days, part of embracing the idea that, with hard work, good things do happen, and they are real, and they can actually last!

Basically, I had to grow into me as I kept growing—or shrinking—if that makes sense. It did to me, anyhow.

One of my sillier but actually serious goals was: I wanted to be able to walk around the house naked. It wasn't because I wanted to flash Tom. In fact, it wasn't even about clothes. It was about getting naked with myself, about being honest and comfortable with who I was at that moment.

Tom thought I was being too hard on myself for having doubts and worries. But then that's me. I have my issues. One morning we were at the kitchen table, and I told him that, a few years ago, I had refused to audition for the wonderfully funny sitcom, *Malcolm in the Middle*, because the opening scene had the mom (played brilliantly by Jane Kaczmarek) vacuuming the living room while topless. It didn't matter that they showed her from the back. I couldn't do it.

I was still horrified whenever I thought about the time Wolfie had seen way too much of me. It had happened a year or so before I lost weight. I was blow-drying my hair in my bathroom. The door, though slightly ajar due to the position of the sink, was for all practical purposes closed, and other than the sound of the blow dryer in my ear I couldn't hear anything, including a knock on the door.

Wolfie later said he had knocked, and maybe he had. Either way, he didn't wait for me to respond. He pushed the door open and barged right into the bathroom, where he came face to face with me as I normally am when I blow-dry my hair: in front of the mirror, with a white terry cloth towel around my waist but nothing on top. Like a wannabe *Venus de Milo*, with arms.

Don't get me wrong. I didn't mind being thought of in the same vein as Aphrodite, the Greek goddess of love and beauty. I just didn't want my boobage admired in person, especially by my son, who gasped, "Oh, my God! I'm sorry, Mom!"

I saw him through a layer of hair. I immediately shut off the blow-dryer, set it on the counter, and pulled up my towel. In my haste, I did more rearranging of my towel than actual covering up of my private parts. I'm pretty sure I managed to expose even more skin.

Wolfie froze. The last time he'd seen my boobs, he was an infant. It was a very different experience for him as a teenager. He swiftly backed out of the bathroom, mumbling another "I'm sorry."

I never found out what he wanted. By the time I finished my hair and got dressed, he had gone to a friend's house. I found Tom and told him that I had just caused my son irreparable harm.

"He's never going to look at boobs the same way again," I said. "I can hear him in twenty years telling his shrink, 'Oh yeah, I remember when I saw my mom naked and my life was never the same.' "

Tom was not sympathetic.

"Hey, V," he said.

"What?"

"My life hasn't been the same since I saw you naked."

"Ha," I said, rolling my eyes.

The truth was, Tom hadn't gotten to see me naked that soon after we started seeing each other. He jokes that, after I'd fall asleep, he'd turn on the light and look. But early in our relationship, I had been extremely self-conscious about taking my clothes off in front of Tom. We had known each other a while before we got intimate. At that point in my life, I wasn't a slow starter as much as I was careful. Ditto Tom, who had four children from a previous marriage and was reluctant to add another person to that complex situation.

My hesitancy, though, was different from his. It was all mind-body related. As much as I liked him and wanted to be with him romantically, I wondered how he could fall in love with me when I didn't love myself. I laughed the first time I saw him naked. He had a fine body, but I was nervous, and I have always dealt with stress by cracking jokes. If he had laughed at me, I would have been devastated.

But he didn't get a chance to see me when I finally stripped to my birthday suit. I made sure the bedroom was dark, the drapes were pulled, and the lights were off. If I hadn't been wrapped around him, he would have needed a seeing-eye dog to find me. Tom was allowed to bump into me, but he couldn't look. It was ridiculous, but it was a process that I needed to go through, and fortunately he was patient enough to put up with me until I quit paying attention to whether the drapes were up or down.

Eventually, I realized the lights had never mattered. It was all about how I saw myself when I shut my eyes and looked at myself from the inside out.

While promoting *Losing It* in different cities, I kept wondering how truly comfortable I was inside my new 132-pound body. It was stupid. I really did like myself better and I was happy with the improvements I had made. I spent all day telling people that, Yeah, I did it and I was proud of myself. And that was true. Yet alone at night in the hotel room, I looked through fashion magazines and battled feelings of inadequacy and fears that I was a fake. I wondered, What the eff was going on?

How could I feel both good about myself and on the verge of a freak out? But hey, as I had to realize, life was full of contradictions and self-doubt, thrills, and victories. I had to get used to the fact that it wasn't always a perfect picture. A diet is a process of gradual change, and even though it had taken ten months to get where I was, this new lighter me was still too new for me to completely accept or trust.

Never mind the fashion magazines. I also had a hard time with the room service menu. Everything I ever fantasized about doing in a hotel room was listed on the left side and the right side of that tall, slender menu. I closed my eyes and imagined ordering up the most illicit threesome: a starter, an entrée, *and* dessert!

Talk about temptation. But that's when I would ask myself which version of myself I liked, the new or the old, the fit or the fat, the size 6 or the size 14; then, drawing on every ounce of will-power and self-discipline, I would order up salmon with NO butter and a side of vegetables, and "please, no bread."

Tom was always helpful on the phone when I was traveling without him, and he offered even more strength when he was with me. I also made sure to stay at hotels with gyms. I had lost weight, but I was still fighting the battle.

Getting naked, as I came to define it, was all about being honest with myself. By the time Wolfie walked in on me in the bathroom, he knew flaws of mine that were worse than any insecurity I had about my body. He had seen me lose my temper, cry from frustration and loneliness, and sit on the couch and stuff my face as if I could never get full. In other words, he had seen way more than my boobs.

We all show more of ourselves than we realize. One time, I pulled off the freeway near my house and stopped at the bottom of the off-ramp. A disheveled man stood off to the side. As soon as we made eye contact, he opened his coat and flashed me. He was completely naked underneath. Shocked, I sped off before waiting for the light to change.

In the aftermath, though, I remembered the pain and desperation in his eyes rather than anything else I saw. He had exposed much more than his body.

When I was on the series *Touched by an Angel*, I wore so many layers of clothing to hide my embarrassing girth that I may as well have been peeling an artichoke at the end of the day when I undressed. But the one thing I could never conceal was the unhappiness in my eyes. To this day, when I'm flipping through channels and come across one of those episodes, I only see my pain. I want to grab that version of me and tell her it's going to get better.

While flying home after one trip, I watched a movie starring Kate Winslet, one of my favorite actresses. Though she kept her clothes on in this particular movie, she frequently got naked onscreen and seemed comfortable showing her body. Clothed or not, she conveys enviable self-confidence. I applaud the way she has spoken out about the importance of looking real, as opposed to emaciated, so that her daughters and others of their generation don't grow up thinking you have to look thin to be beautiful.

Women of my age need that, too. As I had discovered at age 48, feeling healthy and normal has as much to do with being honest with myself as it does with eating right and exercising. When I thought about wanting to walk around the house naked, what I really meant was that I wanted to feel the comfortable confidence that I saw in Kate Winslet's eyes, whether I was dressed or buck naked. To get there would require more than adhering to a diet over the long haul. I would have to be forthright with my emotions, my relationships, and my dealings with other people. I would have to recognize when I felt less than I was, figure out why, and push myself to be better.

Could I do it? It didn't seem like it when I got home after this one trip. I was grateful to be back smelling the familiar smells, sleeping in my own bed, and hearing my cat Dexter purr at night. I fell asleep next to Tom as if he were the missing piece I needed to complete the puzzle. But the next morning we began setting up for a party we were having that weekend, and we got into a fight. It was a first-class blowout that ended up with both of us walking off in separate directions.

Suddenly, I didn't feel very evolved. If anyone were looking for proof that losing weight didn't make me a know-it-all, though I had sounded like one a few days before giving interviews and signing books, here was proof. Wolfie looked up from his video game as I stormed through the living room.

"What's going on?" he asked, but then before I could answer he added, "Are you guys okay?"

"We're having a discussion," I said.

"Yeah," he said with raised eyebrows. "It sounded like you were fighting about how to set up the chairs."

He was right, but I felt like showing my appreciation for his intelligence with a wave of my middle finger. I didn't.

"Are the chairs that big of a deal?" he asked.

"Don't start," I said.

With that, I harrumphed off in another direction. Two things then happened that resolved the strain that permeated our household. First, Tom walked into the kitchen just after I grabbed a large bag of cheddar cheese rice cakes from the pantry. He caught me struggling to break it open. It was one of those bags that resist the most strenuous efforts at breaking the seal, and once he saw what I was doing, I was too embarrassed to rip the bag with my teeth. I would have preferred taking a bite out of Tom instead.

"Oh, really," he said. "That's how you're going to handle this?"

"I'm an emotional eater," I said. "Right now, I'm very emotional—and I'm trying really hard to eat."

"But?"

"I can't open the friggin' bag," I said.

With both gallantry and sensitivity, Tom took the rice cakes from my hands and put them back in the pantry. Then we had one of our best and most honest talks ever. And later that night, I got into bed feeling much more relaxed and at peace, as well as grateful that I had not eaten my way through my anger. Tom slid in a bit later. It took a minute before he noticed the surprise I had for him. He looked under the covers to make sure, then turned to me and said, "Hey, you're naked."

Notes to Myself

❧

If the life I want is in my hands, what happens when I wash them? Does the life I want go away or get cleaner?

Think of the feeling you have after a great workout. Now compare it to the feeling you have after an unhealthy eating streak, with little to no physical activity. Now re-think *going to the gym, the bag of chips,* or whatever your devil seems to be today. The choice becomes a little easier, right?

Here's a big question I'm never going to solve, but I'm wondering about it: Most people have clean or relatively clean bathrooms in their home. Why then are public bathrooms so messy? Does everyone decide to miss the toilet?

I think people can do a little better in general if they take a moment to improve their aim. It 's a good life lesson— something to think about anyway.

Chapter Four

Warning Lights

Whoever said "if you want to make God laugh, make plans" was right—and as a result, I had a problem.

I had a full calendar of out-of-town book signings ahead of me, all of which had been carefully scheduled and coordinated to coincide with Wolfie's Van Halen tour dates. I thought it would be fun if we were in the same cities at the same time. But all the planning turned out to be for naught when the band suddenly cancelled dates at the end of February and all through March while Ed dealt with health issues.

The band put out a statement saying he needed to undergo tests and "determine a defined diagnosis." I didn't ask Wolfie for any additional details. That only put him in a difficult spot. I didn't really want to know either. I had seen him through many hard times in the past. I felt badly for him. I knew how important playing with Wolfie on the tour was to him. I also knew from my own experience that you had to learn to get out of your own way if you wanted to change.

Three weeks later, I was back home between travel dates to celebrate Wolfie's seventeenth birthday. Ed, looking better than I expected, and Janie, joined Tom and Tony and myself at Il Tiramisu, our favorite neighborhood Italian restaurant. I believed we had gone there for Wolfie's birthday the past ten years. None of us could remember exactly. However, we did agree that the owner, Ivo, and his son, Peter, made the best pasta fagioli in the vicinity.

The evening was surprisingly relaxed and warm. At home, after remarking on Ed's fragility, Tom and I recalled our own journeys through tough times. He had struggled through a difficult divorce and I had climbed my way out of the depths of self-punishment. Tom said he always knew that things would work out as long as he followed what he felt in his heart was right and true. I asked how he knew, and he said it was his faith in God.

"I couldn't have made it without my faith," he said.

My first reaction was to think, really? I was different. I had needed to find faith in myself before I could think about whether it also involved a Higher Power. Of course, now I found myself thinking about and talking to God all the time. But I remembered the way it had been.

"You know what I did during my darkest days?" I asked. "I ate."

"What got you to turn things around?" he asked.

"I had to," I said. "I knew I couldn't go on any longer the same way. All the proverbial reasons."

Tom scratched his head.

"Did you think God was helping you?" he asked.

"All I know is that nobody is helping me when I'm running on that damn treadmill," I said.

"Come on, V. Seriously."

"Honestly, I wish I knew God the way you do."

"Well, you like the way I know the Bible," he said.

"I do."

"I have head knowledge," he said. "You have the knowledge in your heart."

That caused me to pause.

"I'm open, I'm curious," I said. "I've only had a very few times in my life that I would call spiritual, where I've felt a connection with a higher power. For whatever reason, though, I don't have that same thing in me where I can blindly believe."

"Then how do you know right from wrong? In a way where you answer to a higher authority?"

"I don't know that I answer to any authority higher than my conscience," I said.

"How do you know if you're doing anything wrong?"

"A warning light goes on inside me."

"Seriously."

"I'm being serious."

"When you think of being at peace with yourself and the world, what comes to mind? What are you looking for?"

"How would you answer that?"

"I'm looking for God," Tom said. "But I asked you."

I closed my eyes and thought. It was a good question.

"I guess I'm looking for my grandmother's soup," I said.

"V"—

"I'm serious," I said. "*Cappelletti in brodo*. Mmmm. My memory of that soup is as close to a religious experience as I have."

"You're serious?"

"Absolutely," I said. "I think everyone has something like that in their life, something that makes time stop, problems melt away, and everything seem perfect. It's not soup for everyone. For some people, it might be a hike through the redwoods. For someone else, it could be the ritual of a church service. For me, it was *cappelletti in brodo*. I was only seven or eight when I last ate it, but I can recall every nuance of its taste as if it was yesterday. The broth. The cappelletti. I swear it was sublime. I was in heaven. It was love in a bowl."

"Where can I get some?" he asked.

"Never mind you," I said. "Where can *I* get some?"

I flew out of town the following day for a book signing, leaving Tom and the boys at home. I called that night, grumpy and tired. I wished Wolfie had been in town as planned, and I was upset at myself for having told Tom that I would be okay traveling without him. Truth be told, I was lonely. I wasn't tired and I didn't want to watch TV, and it was dreary to go from a store full of people telling me how much they liked and admired me to an empty hotel room.

Tom sympathized long enough for his concern to seem genuine. But I could tell by his voice that he was more interested in letting me know that he had taken our new but unreliable Audi to his favorite service station and had confirmed his suspicions that it was a lemon.

We already had known it was a loser car. We had bought the Q7 about a year earlier and had taken it back to the dealer for repairs more times than either of us wanted to talk about. That car was the source of many debates. I accepted the problems as part of the car's personality. Things went wrong all the time, but so what? I wrote that off as being quirky. I had stayed in a bad marriage for twenty years. I wasn't going to bail on a car that was less than a year old.

My attitude frustrated Tom almost as much as the car itself. *Almost.* His attitude toward cars was entirely different. He railed about it being a lemon and cited California state lemon laws, while I refused to engage in such definitive name-calling lest it hurt the Q7's feelings. He especially loathed the Audi dealership and the manager of the service department, who, he said, refused to "get it."

"The steering wheel has broken six times in the up position," he ranted. "It keeps recurring. Why do they seem surprised each time I bring it in? Something is clearly defective with this particular automobile."

When he used the word "automobile," I knew he was really annoyed. Secretly, I enjoyed seeing him go on about the car and the service people. I thought he was cute. He reminded me of Pat Harrington in *One Day at a Time.* Tom was my handyman, my Schneider.

But he had a point. Eventually, even I couldn't deny or debate it. Now that I was out of town, he had gotten a second opinion at the service station where he takes his truck. As Tom told me on the phone that night, the chief mechanic had pronounced it a lemon.

"No question about it," Tom said, definitively. "It's so sour it could've been the twist in my vodka and soda."

I believed him and promised that I would go with him when he took the Audi back to the dealer to ask that they give us a replacement. But the diagnosis didn't really surprise me. In fact, had I been a jealous woman, I would have been worried as soon as I heard Tom say that he took the car to his favorite service station. Was it a coincidence that he had gone there the day I went out of town?

I already knew he had a total "bromance" going with the chief mechanic. Their relationship had begun when he started working on Tom's truck, which then had 98,000 miles and continues to purr at 160,000-plus. They hit it off immediately, thanks to a similar philosophy about service. Tom referred to service as "maintenance," and apparently the two of them applied the concept to almost all of life, certainly enough of it for them to talk with each other endlessly. Ergo their male bonding.

But then he brought it home to me. It was akin to his showing up with lipstick from another woman on his shirt collar. Except it was a grease stain and it was all about how Manuel, his buddy at the service station, agreed with him. Personally, I didn't want to hear about how cool and smart Manny was and how the two of them had used cars to figure out the key to life.

I'm sure my annoyance stemmed from the fact that I didn't adhere to their . . . well, you might call it a fundamentalist belief in regular maintenance. My more lackadaisical approach irritates Tom, who regularly tries to lecture me, as he did when I returned home from this most recent trip. He couldn't help himself. It was like preaching to the unconverted.

"See, Val, I take care of my cars," he said. "I service them regularly. I don't wait for the light to go on."

"But that's how I and most people know there's something wrong—or that it's time to take the car in."

"That's my point," he said. "By then it's too late. I'm talking about preventive medicine."

"Got it," I said, hoping to end the discussion there even though I knew that was unlikely.

"Aside from the Q, which is a lemon, we don't have a lot of car breakdowns. Right?"

I nodded.

"And why is that?" he asked.

"Because you're in love with the guy at the service station."

"Very funny, but not quite," Tom said, smiling briefly. "It's that both of us believe in preventing stuff before it happens. If you replace worn parts or take care of a rattle or strange noise before they give you a problem—"

"*If* is the operative word," I interrupted.

Tom knew what I meant. He scratched his head in thought, deciding whether or not to continue explaining his point with a metaphor that had, as far as I was concerned, run out of gas. He made the wrong decision. He kept going.

"You're a perfect example," he said. "Your marriage."

"Watch it—"

"Okay, never mind your marriage. Your weight."

"Watch it—"

"No, wait, hear me," he said. "How many years did you allow yourself to eat and gain weight before you did something about it? How many years before you realized you couldn't keep going the same way?"

"I get it."

"See, V, you're a procrastinator."

"Really? Thank you, Mr. Moto."

"How many years was your warning light on before you did anything?"

He had a point, but I refused to say anything more. I looked at him and nodded in complete and utter amazement. I almost felt like applauding. He appeared to be very satisfied with himself. I could picture him at the service station the next day, telling his buddy that he had set me straight about taking care of cars and life in general. I loved him for it, and yet I also wondered what it was that I liked about men.

The next week, Tom and I left for another stint on the road promoting my book. The tour was like being in a state of suspended animation. It was surreal to go someplace and meet hundreds of wonderful people who just wanted to say hello and tell me how much they had enjoyed my work or been inspired by me. Except for one or two creepy stalkerlike guys, people were wonderful and warm. At one bookstore, a woman showed up with a container of gazpacho.

"Why gazpacho?" I whispered to Tom, who had spoken to her. Tom shrugged.

"She said it was delicious."

"But soup at a book signing?"

"We don't know her," he said. "I don't think we should have any."

I agreed and went back to signing books. A few minutes later, Tom returned to the table where I sat. He leaned close enough so that I could smell garlic on his breath as he whispered in my ear.

"You didn't?" I asked.

"She was such a nice woman," he said. "And it was incredible. I saved some for you to have later."

Each stop was like that. They put me on a high. How could they not? Then I would return to the hotel room, look at Tom or glance at myself in the mirror, and think, Really? What am I not getting?

But people saw something I didn't see at the time. They genuinely wanted to connect, and more than that they wanted information and answers. I was reminded of the famous coffee shop scene in *When Harry Met Sally*, when an older woman played by Estelle Reiner watches Meg Ryan's character feign an orgasm and then tells the waitress, "I'll have what she's having."

I was delighted to talk about my diet and wanted everyone to have the same success. I had a hard time, though, whenever someone asked, "What's next for you?"

"Maintenance," I would respond, but then I would fall silent, pretending that was the complete answer even though I knew it wasn't. I didn't know what else to say. They would nod as if they understood. In the meantime, I would find myself thinking about Tom's damn car analogy. Maybe I would just keep going till a warning light came on.

Or would I? As Tom pointed out, even with proper warnings I couldn't be trusted. For instance, he got on me for not having made a dentist appointment for months even though I had a tooth that hurt off and on. He also wondered why I had continually put off seeing my asthma doctor, given the complaining I did about breathing whenever I stepped up my exercise. Then we walked through the front door at home to myriad problems, including a broken air conditioner, a back stairwell that looked further decayed from dry rot, and new cracks along the living room walls.

"Is that crack bigger?" I asked.

"I quit looking a year ago," Tom said, shaking his head disgustedly.

"Hmmm," I said.

As Tom headed into another room, I heard him say something. I couldn't quite make it out, though.

"What'd you say?" I asked.

"Nothing." Then he cleared his throat and added, "Nothing about maintenance."

• • •

A few nights later, I was awakened in the middle of the night by a strange, scary noise. I listened and then nudged Tom until he propped himself up on one elbow and listened with mounting curiosity. We agreed that it sounded like dead bodies groaning from underground, even though neither of us had ever heard that sound.

Moments later, we were in the backyard, following the noise down the hill toward the swimming pool. All sorts of wild animals make their way through our backyard day and night, including deer, coyotes, bobcats, raccoons, skunks, and other creatures I didn't want to think about. In the dark, Tom tried umpteen ways to scare me. He succeeded each time, too.

Despite such creepy thoughts, both of us suspected that a problem with the pool was responsible for the noise. It had been leaking water for three years. Ordinarily, I kept a hose in it on a slow trickle, which I knew was terrible for both the water shortage plaguing the city and my water bill. But apparently someone had turned it off while we were out of town and the water level had dropped to the point where the filter had started sucking in more air than water, and was making the hideous noise that had awakened us.

"Phew, that's a relief," I said after Tom flipped the filter off.

"What is?" he asked.

"We don't have dead bodies groaning underground."

"We have a dead pool instead," he said.

As we walked inside and got back into bed, I knew that I was experiencing a massive lesson in maintenance. Directly and indirectly, I was being shown that it could be difficult whether it had to do with weight, cars, or a house. Had I thought about it, I would have seen that I had hit my goal when I bought the house, when I purchased that Q7, and when I lost 40 pounds; and I would have realized that in each case those were the easy parts. The upkeep was much harder. It didn't end.

This was all a metaphor for a much bigger lesson I was supposed to learn: take action earlier and not wait until there was a problem.

I had to have my own "Holy shit" moment before I got the message. Until then, I had my ever-vigilant boyfriend, who was more than happy to keep me on track. Tom rolled into the kitchen one afternoon looking pleased with himself. The only thing he liked better than having things under control was explaining to me exactly what he had done to get everything in its rightful place, and this was one of those moments. He had just come back from the Audi dealer. They had finally taken back our lemon, but because we loved the car itself, Tom had negotiated for a new Q7.

He led me outside to see it. He ran his hand across the side like a salesman proud of the shine and then opened the door so I could get a whiff of that wonderful new car smell.

"It's nice," I said.

"Want to know something even better?" he asked.

"I do."

"I figured out why I'm in your life," he said.

"Why?" I asked.

"It's so I can tell you when your warning lights are on."

Notes to Myself

❦

Ed came over to pick up Wolfie and take him to rehearsal. I was glad to see he looked good. He talked about himself for an hour. Never mind me hosting a talk show. What about Ed?

As he packed to go back on the road, I asked Wolfie if he had taken enough underwear. Tom chimed in, "He's a rock star now. You need to be more concerned about girlfriends and groupies taking his underwear off." Then, of course, I smashed Wolfie's guitar over Tom's head.

I discovered that people other than me think of the grocery store as a holy place. Today I saw a woman in the produce department holding up a head of cauliflower as she asked, "God, do you think anyone will eat this?"

What if losing weight meant getting rid of the "weight" we carry on our shoulders and inside?

Chapter Five

Blended, Not Stirred

One afternoon before Wolfie left to go back on tour, Tom came downstairs from the boys' room making a face and shaking his head in a way that I knew meant trouble. Neither Wolfie nor Tony was home, so I couldn't imagine the reason, other than maybe he had found cigarettes, booze, or drugs, which he quickly assured me he hadn't. It was worse: he had gone into the boys' bathroom. Sparing me most of the details, he simply termed it a disaster.

"They pee like horses," he said. "I mean, I've heard about blended families. But it doesn't have to be in puddles on the floor!"

"Gross!" I squealed.

"Seriously, it's like using a water cannon on a house plant. Would it be bad if I asked them to sit on the toilet?"

I looked up at Tom with a blank stare. He had asked one of the few questions that could render me silent. Not about the guys sitting on the toilet, which seemed like something he needed to talk to them about among themselves. But the implicit question was about how best to have your kids live together. Ordinarily, I have plenty to say when the subject turns to blended families. Long before Wolfie was born and even more so afterward, I was clear that family is the most important thing in my life. I have been quoted often as saying that motherhood is my favorite role. When I met Tom, who has four children, the part got way more complicated.

In fact, after Tom's rant about the pee in the boys' bathroom, my thoughts suddenly lit on the plans I still needed to make before his children arrived for spring break. I feared that if anything was going to cause me to lose control in the kitchen late one night (hey, the warning light was on!), it would be the stress of dealing with all those kids.

Mind you, much of this stress was self-imposed. From the moment Tom told me that he had four children, which he shared on the night we met, I told myself that I wanted to be the best stepmom in the world. I would bet that a lot of women in similar situations say the same thing. But I may as well have decided to become an astronaut, too. It was impossible. There were too many complications. Five years later, I just wanted to come out a survivor, with my sense of humor and waistline intact.

The first summer that the kids stayed with us, I was determined to make every day spectacular. I made pancakes for them in the morning and three-course meals for lunches and dinners. When they arrived the next summer, I put cereal on the table for breakfast, served sandwiches for lunch, and hoped for a hot dinner at night. By the third summer, I was out of recipes. I let everyone make his or her own breakfast, and midway through their visit I groaned, "They're staying the whole summer?"

•   •   •

Now, as we looked ahead to the fourth summer, I had nothing planned. But in my heart I knew without a doubt that I loved the children. Tom's oldest, Tony, had moved in with us midway through his junior year of high school. He quickly grew close to Wolfie, who surprised me by immediately adjusting from his previous existence as an only child. Rather than have separate bedrooms, they moved two beds into one large room. Tony also plays the bass, and the two of them jam endlessly.

Tom's youngest, Dominic, now ten, is an adorable, energetic boy who walks on the balls of his feet. He's always ready to play or snuggle. But he's the only boy in history who hates French fries. He doesn't like cheese either. Yet he loves quesadillas. Go figure.

Next up is Angela, the family's Italian beauty. When we are out in public, people mistake her for my daughter. An A student, she has the preternatural savvy of a child who grew up quickly. She's fourteen going on twenty-four. Then there's Andie, a coltish seventeen-year-old with the biggest eyes and best legs I have ever seen. She has a passion for creative writing and a fascinating imagination that has Tom and me wondering how she will use it as an adult.

Their hugs at the start of those summer visits put me in the best mood. The problems began a few hours later when everyone wanted to know where they were sleeping and what we were doing for fun the next day. It was typical family stuff, except it involved seven people with seven different agendas. Invariably someone whined that he or she was bored, someone else carped about not liking dinner, and after dinner there were too many people of different ages for everyone to agree on one movie.

Life under one roof like that was a challenge. But it was, in many ways, an even bigger challenge when the other three kids were in

Arizona, looking to Tom for advice or help or the kind of everyday dad stuff that kids want and need. Long-distance parenting strains everyone. I wish I had a dollar for every time I looked at Tom and said, "So you had such a bad marriage that you had four kids."

Gradually my attitude changed. I toughened up, didn't worry as much, and became more realistic about what I could do and what I *would* do for the kids. I knew I couldn't be perfect. No one is—except Mary Poppins, and her calling card said she was *practically* perfect. I came to realize that one day as I was preparing three different versions of dinner, trying too hard to make everyone happy. As I told Tom, I would have been better off letting everyone be miserable, like me.

Hee hee.

After losing weight, I realized that I had changed even more. I didn't want to pretend to be anyone I wasn't. In a way, that was part of the work I still had to do. I may have come out of hiding after losing 40 pounds, but I still had to figure out who that person was, and that didn't change even when we had the kids.

Their most recent visit was one of the hardest, and best. It was their spring break, and for me the challenges began right away. Within a few hours, they had devoured all the food in the fridge and pantry, sending me off on the first of numerous trips to the grocery store, not a place someone who has made national news for losing weight wants to be seen two or three times a day.

I had trouble gauging how much food four teenagers and one ten-year-old boy consumed in a day. It was more than my three Jenny meals and two snacks, that's for sure. Yet I also found my frequent trips to the supermarket a convenient and comforting escape from Tom and his kids as they reconnected, which could be noisy. I wondered if I was still using food to deal with stress even though I wasn't eating it. But I returned home without having given in to temptation.

Then one night Andie engaged Tom in an emotional talk about his divorce. She didn't understand his side of the split. She didn't think that he had gone through any hard times or suffered any pain. From what I observed, it seemed as if she thought that he had waltzed straight into my life. She seemed to want an apology or perhaps an explanation from him.

They ended up having a heartfelt, honest talk. She had forgotten the difficulties that Tom had gone through, how he had been sleeping on a friend's floor when I met him. She didn't know that he had considered himself a failure. Tom told her as much as she could handle, calling it the lowest part of his life. His had been a painful passage that many divorced parents know well.

I stayed out of it, but in spite of their tear-filled, painful back and forth, it was nice to see them connect. Bertinellis keep everything inside and stew in private. If it had been me, I would have buried my head in a pot of marinara sauce. Indeed, even though I was only an observer, I still felt like doing something similar. But I didn't—and that fact was a healthy break from old bad habits.

The next day was better. The kids' friends came over and Tom's sister, Angela, came out from Ohio, her trip having been arranged months earlier. The timing was perfect. She was almost eleven years older than Tom. The kids love her. And I felt like I had a partner. She amused the children with stories of having changed Tom's diapers when he was a baby, and she reminded them of the excellent father they had forgotten. All of them shared some beautiful memories.

I had wanted to strangle them three days earlier. Now I told them that they were adorable and hugged them before they went to bed. I realized that all of us, at our various ages, were trying to get to know ourselves better. We weren't necessarily lovable all the time, but we definitely had our moments.

As always, the best days of their visit came at the end. By this time, everyone had gotten used to one another, found their comfort zone in the house, relaxed, and figured out how to stay in touch with friends back home. Wolfie and Tony took the girls with them on errands. They hung out at the pool, went to the beach, listened to music, and swapped songs on their iPods. It was as if the entire house had exhaled.

After dinner, the kids got up at the same time to play Wolfie's Wii. Without being told, each one of them cleared their plates from the table, thanked me for dinner, and disappeared into the living room, leaving Tom and me alone in the kitchen. I couldn't believe it.

"Whoa," I said. "What just happened?"

"I don't know," he said. "But let's not say anything in case we ruin it."

Later that night, Tom and I were still in the living room, talking with his sister about the kids, who had gone off to their rooms and were either sleeping or watching TV. I wanted to go to bed but was too tired to get up off the couch. A few years earlier, I had been one woman with one child. Now I was exhausted. I jokingly asked Tom and his sister how that had happened. Even better, why had I let it happen?

"Because you met me and I'm irresistible," Tom said.

"You're half right," I said with a laugh.

I tried to look on the positive side. I had stayed on my meal plan. With a house full of people there was no place to sneak off to with a bag of chips or cookies without someone seeing me.

Smiling, Angela warned me not to be hard on myself and reminded us that the kids were really good children. They were resilient and depended on parents having the same kind of ability to bounce back with kindness, understanding, and love. I saw her point. As the week had gone on, I had sensed a change in my attitude toward the kids, including Wolfie. I had let go and become more Zen-like. They could figure out how to amuse themselves and make their own sandwiches.

As much as I loved the kids, I also wanted time for myself. Angela assured me that was normal.

"It's called self-preservation," she said, cracking us up.

Early the next morning, we said goodbye to Tom's sister. Later, Tom put his children on a plane back to Arizona. Wolfie went to his dad's. The house was quiet. I walked through feeling like a storm had passed and savored the solitude at the kitchen table with a cup of coffee and the crossword. Then Tom came in looking sad after I made a remark about everyone being gone. He pretended to wipe a tear.

"Cry all you want," I said. "But I'm happy to have a rest."

"It's not what you think," he said.

"No?"

"Don't hate me. But I emotionally ate."

"Huh? I don't get it."

"On the way back from the airport, I stopped at Burger King," he said.

"That's why you're upset? I thought it was the kids."

He shook his head and added, "I had fries, too."

"Oh, Lord," I said. "I just got rid of five kids. You're going to have to butch it up, babe."

Notes to Myself

Hello to a new day!

Mel Brooks once said, "As long as the world is turning and spinning, we're going to be dizzy and make mistakes." Likewise, as long as the world includes cheeseburgers and chocolate, we're going to find reasons not to eat salads and fruit.

Don't get stuck thinking too long-term. Just think about today, and tomorrow, think about tomorrow. But always remember where you put the TV remote control.

Chapter Six

Catch a Wave

Before one of Wolfie's shows, I took my mom and my dad aside and read them the passage from my first memoir, *Losing It*, about when their second child, a boy, died at two years old after drinking poison that had been stored in a Coke bottle. Since it was something that had rarely been mentioned when I was growing up, I was nervous about revealing this dreadful time in their lives, and even after my book was published, we hadn't talked about this family tragedy much.

After I finished, though, my mom wiped a tear from her eye and thanked me for handling it with sensitivity. She also offered up a few more details about what had happened and how she and my dad had dealt with their unimaginable loss. For her, a woman who rarely speaks about herself, that was equivalent to speaking volumes.

But at seventy-one, my mom was teaching me that it was never too late to change. She was more open and willing to talk than she had been when I was younger. I assumed it was because she now liked herself more than at any other time in her life.

She was also taking better care of herself. About seven years earlier, she had been diagnosed with a heart valve problem and warned that eventually she would need surgery. Motivated to take better care of herself, she changed her diet, lost some weight, and gradually improved her lifestyle.

As she saw the progress I made on Jenny Craig, she went on her own diet. She was typically quiet about it. She didn't announce it to everyone or ask me for advice. She just cut her calories and started to exercise.

Toward the end of 2007, around the same time I reached my goal, she reached out to me for help. She had dropped close to 16 pounds, which was great, but she thought she could do better on Jenny Craig and asked if I could help her. My mom turned out to be my biggest fan, explaining that I had inspired her. She also turned out to be a tad competitive.

"Val, if you can do it, I think I can handle it, too," she said with a playful chuckle.

"Hey, what's that supposed to mean?" I asked.

"It means the apple doesn't fall far from the tree," she said.

My mom was so right—more than I cared to admit. As a young woman, she had been drop-dead beautiful. Her wedding photos still take my breath away. However, by the time I was in my teens and twenties, she had lost that figure and dressed in large, formless A-style dresses, the same thing I had done when I had packed on the pounds, except that I wore over-sized men's dress shirts.

Both of us had been hiding our pain under our weight and big clothes. At eight years old, my mother had lost her mother and she had had to learn to soldier on without complaint. She handled the loss of her child the same way. Later, as she raised four children while my dad, a retired GM executive, rose up the ranks, there were issues in her marriage. At each juncture, walls went up—and gradually so did her weight.

I had resented her for not taking better care of herself. Now, of course, I looked back and saw that my anger was incredibly selfish and self-centered. How dare I be offended at her for not being the way I wanted her to be! Fortunately, our communication skills had improved since then.

Of course, I got her on Jenny Craig and she embraced the program. One day I called and she said she had just finished riding her stationary bike. She said she'd pedaled for forty minutes and was working up to an hour. She wanted to know how long I exercised for each day. I knew what she was doing, because I did it myself, and I reminded her that dieting wasn't a competition.

"I have more weight to lose than you," she said.

"Maybe now," I said. "But I've just spent a year working my ass off."

"And now I'm doing the same thing." She laughed.

Her determination impressed me, especially at her age. But she explained that age was her biggest motivator. She wanted to feel better and healthier. She mentioned her heart problem. She said she heard the ticking of the clock. As she knew, at some point, she would need surgery.

Well, I didn't like to hear her talk that way. She told me to shush and be real about things. By getting fitter, she increased her chances of an easier recovery, not to mention bettering the odds of surviving the operation.

"I wish I'd done this sooner," she said.

"I'm glad you're doing it now," I said.

I remember when she called to let me know that she had lost another five pounds. She was bursting with pride. I knew the feeling. I smiled.

"You go, Mom!" I said.

"I don't care if you're nineteen or ninety," she said. "You have to want to do it—and I do. I'm not ready to go yet."

"Glad to hear that," I said.

We kept trading information and encouragement. I liked the way we were talking to each other. It might have sounded superficial, a mother and daughter discussing their diets, but as I came to realize, we were relating to each other differently and more positively. For the first time, we were able to open up and talk.

I finally saw my mom as a woman with her own full and complex life, and in her own way, she felt similarly about me. It was no coincidence that each of us felt better about ourselves.

She called one day after seeing me on TV to let me know she was pleased to see me "out of my cocoon," as she put it, "And no longer hiding out at home and making excuses that you had to take care of Wolfie."

"I did?" I asked.

"It's like you rejoined the world."

"You, too," I said.

In January, I was at my parents' house and noticed several brochures for cruises on the coffee table. I picked one up as a distraction from the heated political debate we were having. My dad and I were like fire and gasoline when we talked politics. He was a Bill

O'Reilly–loving conservative who backed McCain-Palin for president and didn't care that I was vacillating between Hillary and Obama because he thought both were the wrong choice.

"I refuse to get involved," my mom said. "I just know your dad and I feel everybody in California is way too liberal."

"That's getting involved," I said.

"No, I'm not taking sides," she said. "But we have to get this country back on track."

"We aren't going to solve it here," my dad said.

"All I want to say is that Bush is probably better off on his ranch," my mom added.

"Amen," I said.

Although presidential politics turned us into a bunch of bickering talk radio rejects, we were in total agreement about the progress my mom was making on her diet. Since going on Jenny Craig, she had dropped 19 pounds. Added to the 16 she had already lost, she had shed a total of 35 pounds. She rode her stationary bike daily for an hour while watching a DVD player she perched on a nearby stool. She had gone down a couple of dress sizes. She joked about taking off another five pounds, which would bring her total to 40 pounds, like mine.

"Maybe I'll keep going," she said, shaking her head confidently.

"Me, too," I said, with a wink.

In all seriousness, I let her know that she looked great.

"When you're young, dieting is about looks," she said. "At my age, it's about making it to the next age."

"I'm with you, Mom," I said. "It should always be about health and feeling good."

In February, mom's weight loss caught the eye of a Jenny Craig executive and at the end of the month they put her in a commercial with me. We shot the ad on a soundstage in front a fruit-and-vegetable stand designed to make it look like we were shopping. I explained that my mom and I, after losing weight, were now "a size energetic."

Then she tugged on my arm and said, "Come on, Val, keep up." She was adorable.

Afterward, we went out to dinner. Despite the dangers of talking politics, we ended up back on the subject of who we should elect as president. This time, I decided to take advantage of my parents' new openness. I knew they had supported Kennedy in 1960 when we lived in Claymont, Delaware. I asked when they had switched from Democrats to Republicans.

I was surprised to find out that my mom had done a lot more than support JFK. She had been the secretary of the Claymont Democratic Club. After Kennedy's win over Richard Nixon, she attended a special celebration for volunteers at the White House, where the new president thanked each of them personally.

"Did you meet him?" I asked.

"He spoke to the group," she said. "A few people might have met him individually. I didn't."

"But you were right there with him," I said.

"He was very good-looking," she smiled. "I wish that I would have tried harder to shake his hand."

As for Lyndon Johnson, my mom said she thought he was second rate ("not good enough," she said) and then, after glancing at my dad, she laughingly said that Nixon was even worse. He agreed. They had voted for Bill Clinton the first time, something my dad admitted so grudgingly I found it funny.

"But after Monica Lewinsky, no, we couldn't continue to support him," my mom said.

I looked at my dad.

"No comment," he said.

"Valerie, this may surprise you," my mom said.

"What?"

"If Hillary wins the nomination, I may support her."

"You're kidding!" I said.

"I want to hear more," my mom said. "I'm definitely intrigued."

"Are you kidding?" I asked.

"Never say never," she shrugged. "You have to keep an open mind."

I stared at her in disbelief. Was this really my mom? She brightened the table with a satisfied grin. I marveled at her and thought, as I had done so often lately, you go girl.

In mid March, I went with Tom and Wolfie to Hawaii to shoot another new Jenny Craig commercial. This one celebrated the fact I had reached my weight loss goal by showing me catching a wave on a surfboard. I loved the symbolism of being 40 pounds lighter and able to finally lift myself up. I really wanted to convey the joy I felt.

I also hoped I could stand up on the board. For several days, I practiced with Mark, my surf instructor. I loved feeling fit and strong in the water. It was a new experience for me. It was fun. As I said in the commercial, I may have weighed less in my twenties, but I didn't feel as energetic.

I stayed in the water for hours, practicing my surfing skills. I wanted to feel what I could do in my body. I also wanted to get it right. The *Rachel Ray Show* had also sent a crew to get behind-the-scenes footage, and they were getting a lot of scenes of my behind crashing into the water.

"I'm just going to get up and fall down and get up and fall down," I complained to Tom and Wolfie.

"You're in Hawaii," Tom said. "What's the problem?"

"Mom," Wolfie said, putting his arm around me. "You're going to do great. There's nothing to worry about—except getting eaten by a shark."

"Thanks a lot."

"No, seriously," he said. "Just keep practicing and you'll do it."

He was right. After I was given a long and very stable surfboard, I was able to stand up time after time. I was only riding one and two footers, but hey, the point was to surf—and I was doing it!

For me, the best part was hearing Wolfie cheer for me. As I shot the commercial, I could hear his and Tom's voice carry over the waves. Several times, a few people jokingly suggested I slip into bikini and show off my new size surfer girl body. I recoiled in horror. I was, like, hell no. Why would I want to ruin a perfectly wonderful trip to Hawaii?

And it was a wonderful trip. Tom and I took long romantic walks on the beach, and I had some pretty great conversations with Wolfie about the tour, his girlfriend, and where he was in his life. It was the kind of conversation that I'd never had with my mom at that age. Thirty years later, we were just learning how to talk to each other.

Before dinner on our last night on the island, Wolfie gave me a hug so big that he literally picked me up off the ground. He was congratulating me on being a successful surfer girl.

"You did good, Ma!" he said.

I looked at him and thought maybe he was right, maybe I was doing good.

Notes to Myself

✂

Since when did the four basic food groups become meat, fruit, vegetables, and dairy? I always thought they were Italian, Chinese, sushi, and Mexican.

Think before you act. Good advice, though in my case, I have to think again about what I just thought.

Here's a logical progression: be accountable for the food you eat, be accountable for the words you speak, be accountable for the life you live.

Chapter Seven

Forgiveness (Spring Cleaning)

A few weeks after we got back from Hawaii, I cleaned out my closet. I always clean it out when I need to regroup and reground myself. It's not an activity I plan or mark on the calendar; it's more of a spontaneous action after I spend a few days or weeks telling Tom and anyone else within earshot that I need to clean out my closet.

In truth, I never *need* to clean it. My closet is always pretty neat and organized. In fact, I built it myself—thank you, Ikea and Hold Everything! But somehow I'm drawn to the activity with a weird predictability that makes me think I might have a genetic predisposition or may have been a chambermaid in another life. This time, as I was cleaning, purging, and rearranging, I realized that this exercise had little to do with cleaning. It was about forgiveness.

I had actually started this round of cleanup before we went to Hawaii, jumping in under the guise of finding some cute sundresses and fun outfits to take on the trip. Instead I had spent a couple of days poking around in there, as time permitted, pulling out a few of the size 14s and 12s and 10s that still lingered on hangers. I looked at them with the surprise of seeing an old classmate, like, what are you doing here? Of course, I was only fooling myself. I knew that, despite my weight loss and public declarations of never returning to life as a size fattie, I had kept them *just in case.*

I didn't like living with that "just in case" excuse—either in the back of my head or the back of my closet. It was an invitation to failure. Six months earlier, I had cleaned most of my closet thinking that I'd never need those larger sizes again. I had told myself, "Leap—and the net will follow."

How big of a leap was I really making if I had labeled a tiny portion of my closet "Just in case" or "Remember when"? It was like keeping a bag of M&Ms in a jar with a sign that said, "Break Glass in Case of Emergency." No, thanks.

So I began removing those items that had migrated steadily from the center of the closet to the fringes where the light never shined. Interrupted by the Hawaii trip, I started back on the closet after we had settled back into a routine. And since I'd been thinking a lot about the concept of maintenance and all that it included, my mindset was different this time. I realized that I was doing more than getting rid of old clothes. I was saying goodbye to the memories I associated with each pair of pants, each dress, each blouse.

I still had some of the "fat" clothes I had purchased when I lived in Park City while working on *Touched by an Angel* and eating myself into a sad stupor every night. One look at those clothes and I was reminded how they were all about covering up and hiding. Next to them were several size 14s I had worn over Christmas

2004, the first holiday I had spent with Tom and we had played touch football with all the kids and my knees had ached after fifteen minutes from my being heavy and out of shape.

I also saw an outfit that I remembered wearing years earlier when I'd had a fight with Ed. Down the rack were clothes that provided more memories, including a two-week period when I was apart from thirteen-year-old Wolfie and had to hear about his homework over the phone. If I shut my eyes, I can remember working all day and then running through the Salt Lake airport to catch a plane home.

Then, as I was about to say, enough, a dress seemed to jump out at me. On closer look, I saw it still had a tag. It was a size miserable and it immediately took me back to those dismal times when I had lain in bed at night in front of the TV, lonely, depressed, isolated, and feeling that this was the rest of my life and I wasn't ever going to be loved or feel love again, and wasn't worthy of it either.

I took it out of the closet. I wanted to look at it in the light. It was huge. Worse, it reminded me of something my mother might have worn years ago.

"Oh Jesus, I said to myself. "I was turning in my mom."

I didn't say it as a criticism of her. It was a revelation. My mom, who was undergoing her own transformation, didn't even want to be that version of herself.

Finally, I packed all those clothes and their memories in boxes, took them to the donation box, and wished them luck. I no longer needed them or wanted the emotional crap I associated with them. Goodbye, good riddance, good luck. The museum of misery, once also known as my closet, was now closed.

Afterward, I grabbed Tom's arm and led him through the

house, looking for more things to pack up and donate. I wanted to maintain the high. I gushed about feeling that I had a clean slate, a fresh start.

"Did you get rid of everything?" he asked.

"Not everything," I said. "I kept all the clothes I've worn in the past Jenny commercials."

"And?"

I shrugged.

"I don't know that I'll ever be completely done."

In fact, with that statement, I had a feeling that I was finally starting to figure out the idea of maintenance. I wish I had gotten it earlier, like when I was helping Wolfie practice his driving, and arguing with Tom about warning lights. And maybe I had gotten it then, too; maybe that was all part of the process of getting to this new point of more clarity.

Unlike a diet, with its simple formula of eating fewer calories and getting more exercise, maintenance isn't as easily defined. Most people, including me, understand it to mean not regaining the weight that we had lost, but maybe not everyone knows that it also means that we have to keep working with change.

I decided that maintenance also has to do with cleaning closets. A diet is only the first step. We have to keep cleaning to remain successful, just as we need to keep ourselves open to the process of change that helped us lose that weight, which will help us keep it off.

For me, this came as a revelation. I had gradually come to understand that maintenance is influenced a little bit by everything I had been going through, from trying to figure out how to deal with my rapidly maturing son, to rethinking the way I related to my mom, to the drumbeat of change coming from Barak Obama's presidential campaign.

It may have required taking a pile of clothes to Goodwill for me to bring this vision into focus, but one thing became clearer. I liked this new version of me. Even better than being thinner, I liked feeling healthier, and that hadn't happened simply because I had lost weight. It happened because I had changed the way I live. And now I didn't want to stop making changes.

Nor could I. If I wasn't going to use food to deal with issues of insecurity, anger, and anxiety, I had to deal with those issues in some other way.

But where was I supposed to start?

Since I was in Spring Cleaning mode, I decided to focus on forgiveness, the emotional version of cleaning. Why forgiveness? Because I suck at it and needed the practice. Also, I saw it as giving myself and other people permission to not be perfect. It took some of the pressure off. Half jokingly, I told Tom that I was going to start with President Bush and Vice President Cheney.

Then I moved on to forgiving myself for getting fat and punishing myself for things that weren't necessarily my fault, as well as for things that were my fault but that I should have dealt with differently. I forgave myself for having wasted time in a marriage that had fewer good years than the twenty it lasted. I also forgave myself for the time I had wasted feeling sorry, alone, scared, and ashamed. And that was just the start.

I got into the nitty gritty, like my lack of willpower when I smelled butter and garlic. I did more forgiving than a priest working a double shift in a confessional. Then Tom suggested forgiving the grudges I held against other people. I gave him a look that asked, Why would I want to do something that sensible? He quoted Mark 11:25: "And when you stand praying, if you hold anything against anyone, forgive him, so that your Father in heaven may forgive you your sins."

"That's a lot to throw at me," I said.

"It was your idea," he replied.

He had a point—and I had plenty of my own sins that others would need to forgive me for sooner or later. After thinking about it, I did feel better—not entirely, but a little—when I forgave my dad for his support of Bush and Cheney. As for my mom, I had more or less come to terms with her. I had already worked through the things she never talked to me about when I was growing up, like my period or sex, and the way she'd handled it when she learned I was having sex (not well—she'd read about it in my diary and then screamed at me though my locked bathroom door). I also regretted the years I had spent being angry with her for having gained weight. Look what had happened: I'd done the same thing.

It was time to let go and understand that all of us were creatures of habits handed down from our parents and their parents. The people who had taught my parents how to love had also taught them that most of life's problems could be solved with a loaf of garlic bread. My parents then handed the same tendencies down to me.

It's what we knew—until we knew better. Unfortunately, I wasn't able to think as simply when I thought about my oldest brother, Drew.

Drew and I have been estranged for nearly seven years. As I recall it, the rift started when I asked him to move out of my house at the beach, where he'd been living in the guesthouse. My parents, who'd moved to Las Vegas, had also lived there. At the time, I was figuring out my divorce from Ed and thought I might have to sell the place in order to survive on my own. As much as Drew may have understood, he still resented me for that decision.

At the end of that December, I had invited my family to spend the holiday with me in Park City, where I worked on *Touched by an Angel*. Everyone came except for Drew. He called on Christmas and the phone was passed around. But when I got on, he was ice cold. It took me by surprise, so I asked, "Whoa, dude, what's up?" He said, "I'll tell you what's up" and then he tore into me, calling me a fake, a lousy sister, a bad daughter, and a self-centered bitch who pretended to love our parents.

"How can you say that?" I asked.

"You kicked them out of the beach house," he said. "You kicked me out of the beach house. You made promises that you didn't fulfill."

"What are you talking about?"

"You know what I'm talking about," he said.

I broke down sobbing, yet continued to listen to Drew's complaints and criticisms. Finally, my dad grabbed the phone and scolded Drew. My mom then took a turn defending me. By then, it was too late. Everyone was angry, and our lovely family Christmas was ruined.

Afterward, I reminded myself of my version of the truth: that my parents had moved out of the beach house because the cold ocean air bothered my mom's arthritis and my dad hated California's high state taxes, which he swore paid for State Assembly Speaker Willie Brown's expensive suits. As for my brother, yes, I had asked him to move out of the guesthouse in case I had to sell the property, but I was also pissed at him for not taking care of the property the way I thought he should.

In retrospect, maybe I wasn't completely forthright with him. As I thought more about what he had said back then, I had a horrific revelation that he might have been right about some things he'd said. Even though my parents and brothers were defending me in the background at the time, I feared he may have described the real me. Maybe I was all that he had said. My marriage was about to end, I had cheated on Ed, felt unworthy of being loved, and felt just generally worthless. I was at such a low point in my life, why not believe him?

The sting lasted a long time, but eventually I recovered. Sadly, my relationship with Drew didn't. We moved on in separate directions, connected more by anger and hurt feelings than the good times we had shared in the past. At some point, I wondered if maybe we had unintentionally helped each other kick-start the rest of our lives. Maybe pushing him out of the house had forced him to stand on his own. He definitely had forced me to start facing some ugly truths about myself.

About five months before my spring cleaning, Drew's wife, Laura, had e-mailed Tom from their home in Washington, asking for tickets to the Van Halen show that was coming there. They wanted to see Wolfie and Ed. Before the show, Wolfie called me and said, "Uncle Drew is going to be here. What should I do?" I told him not to worry, that it would be nice to see Uncle Drew and Aunt Laura and their kids, Calvin and Bailey.

"I'm sure Uncle Drew won't bite," I said.

A few hours later, he called back and said that my brother had been "really cool." He also said it had been nice to see Aunt Laura and his cousins again.

After years of little to no contact with Drew, I felt better that Wolfie had seen his uncle and cousins, and who knows, maybe there was a thawing of the hard feelings. A week or so later, Wolfie e-mailed me several photos he had taken of Drew and his family. I looked at the pictures and wondered if I would ever try to mend the problem with my brother or if he would reach out to me.

I wasn't ready to do it on my own, but I was open to the idea— and that was a first step. Maybe the next spring one of us would be cleaning out our closet and . . .

Notes to Myself

❧

"Forgiveness is the economy of the heart . . . forgiveness saves the expense of anger, the cost of hatred, the waste of spirits."
—Hannah More

It's important to remember that boredom is not another mealtime.

Our inner life is the place to which we most often escape. Think good thoughts and make it a great one—better than the pantry!

Chapter Eight

Birthday Cake

I showed up in the last place anyone would have expected to see me: a Beverly Hills plastic surgeon's office. I wasn't getting a surgical procedure; don't worry. I was reporting a story for *The Doctors*, a daytime talk show, about "oxygen facials," a new, highly-touted treatment that was supposed to take years off your face. I didn't see years disappear; but it felt wonderful.

Indeed, for the hour that I reclined in the chair and let the technician cleanse my face at close range with atomized moisturizers sprayed through a stream of pressurized oxygen, it was pretty darn heavenly. The technician told me that Madonna swore by the oxygen facial. Good for her. I loved the luxury of having an hour of quiet all to myself while someone washed my face for me. (Too bad I couldn't have someone run the treadmill for me, too.)

Afterward, I marveled at the soft, clean texture of my skin and the way my face glowed. I definitely looked and felt fresher—and that was good. It was April, and as it happens on the twenty-third of that month, I turn a year older. This year would be my forty-eighth. Tom and I planned to celebrate with a nice dinner in New York City since I had to be there for work.

If celebrating a birthday seems antithetical to an actress, or to anyone in these youth-obsessed times, I am happy to start a new trend. I don't worry about how it affects my career. I am happy to act my age. I'm grateful to have been blessed with the looks of a girl next door rather than a sex symbol. It provides job security that isn't as dependent on how young or old I look.

Anyway, the simple reality is, I was going to get a year older whether I liked it or not. I decided to like it. I attributed that healthy outlook to having gotten healthier in general. It was also in keeping with a pragmatism I was trying to apply to maintenance. I would accept the things I couldn't change and work to change the things I felt were unacceptable.

After my oxygen facial, I thought of my grandmother, who lived until she was eighty-eight. I think she spent most of those years standing in the kitchen, kneading dough, and stirring sauces in large pots on the stove. For her, cooking was child-rearing, exercise, and religion all in one. I laughed softly as I walked from the plastic surgeon's office to my car. My grandma wouldn't have understood a facial. I could almost hear her, with total bewilderment, ask, "You pay for someone to do what? Wash your face?"

I couldn't imagine what she would have said about Botox, eye-lifts, and face pulls. Maybe people were better off before they had all those options. Jessica Tandy was gorgeous in her seventies and eighties. As her face changed, she only got more beautiful and interesting. Likewise, Meryl Streep and Frances McDormand, who have shunned the pressure to have work done.

Maybe they heard designer Isaac Mizrahi say, "Do you want to look seventy? Get a facelift." I couldn't agree more. I liked the quote, "Laugh a lot, and when you're older all your wrinkles will be in the right places."

Although I wouldn't stop any woman who hits forty, hears an alarm, and calls Dr. 90210, I would warn her that a nip/tuck won't pacify the demons in her head. At the same time, some problems should be fixed. I faced an issue early in my life. I was barely twenty years old when my hair began to turn gray. At first I thought it was kind of cool, like I was getting more mature. Back then, I was eager to be treated like an adult, not a child. I don't know how I thought gray hair would get me there.

Then a cinematographer pointed out my gray hairs. First it was only one that kept popping up. Then he complained about a whole handful of strands. For some reason, they really annoyed him. He also pointed out a bump on my nose that he had trouble lighting properly. Again, it annoyed him.

What an odd thing to be upset about, I thought. And when I questioned him about it, he said, "I just want to make you beautiful." I remember thinking, How are gray hair and a bump on my nose going to make me ugly?

However, as more gray hairs appeared, I became bothered and self-conscious. I finally made an appointment with my hairdresser to get it colored—I'm talking more than highlights—and ever since, I have had to have my hair colored. At this point, I get it done every twelve days. As a young actress, though, I couldn't have had a career with gray hair, and my self-confidence would've suffered. But I have wondered at times how I might have coped if I hadn't been able to cover it up.

Then again, I deal with that imperfection every twelve days.

It's not like I have ever run away from that issue. Maybe some day I will let myself go natural. Hopefully I will carry it off as elegantly as singer Emmylou Harris, who let herself go gray early and has only become more and more beautiful.

I got hung up on age from talking to women in business meetings or to my friends, many of whom were about to turn fifty or had already passed that milestone. A number of them were rattled by it. Some were open, and others quietly disturbed. But their disappointment wasn't about how they looked or how they had aged or any of the superficial things that magazines would have women believe are important. All were bothered by the same thing—regrets about things they hadn't done or hadn't tried or hadn't accomplished. They felt like they had let too many hopes and dreams go unfulfilled. And I think this is key.

I was like, Hey, stop! It's not too late to change. It's never too late to find the real you.

I realized something about growing up. It takes time. I needed forty-seven years to see that I was, as the Bible says, made "fearfully and wonderfully." As I lost weight, I was excited by the version of me that emerged. I was glad the process had happened gradually. Too fast and I might have been shocked. I certainly would have been unprepared. Although, like everyone else starting a diet, I had dreamed about losing twenty pounds in a week—I mean, why not get it over with quickly—I couldn't have handled more than two or three pounds a week. It wouldn't have stuck. I think my diet worked because of the additional work I did on myself. I needed time to think, cry, talk, sweat, celebrate, and constantly replenish the faith I needed every day to stay focused and strong.

Many of the women I dealt with talked about time as if it were the enemy, which it can be if you get to the end and wish you had more time, or wish you had used it more wisely. But one of the biggest yet most subtle changes I noticed after I began maintenance was in my attitude about time. Time is no longer my enemy. I cherish it more, try to use it wisely, and try to share it with the sense that I am giving away something valuable.

Somehow God has figured this out for us. I'm sure that's why it takes almost ten months for a woman to have a child. You need time to prepare. As thrilled as I was when I got pregnant, I would have been in major trouble without time to get ready. In retrospect, my first three months of morning sickness was a little test. It was God saying, Take a crack at this and let's reassess your attitudes and readiness. If I couldn't handle a few months of nausea, how was I going to handle adolescence?

I used to sneer at all the experts who advised living in the moment. Then I came to realize that a moment is about all I can handle—or want to handle. The past and the future as concepts are way too big to grasp. But within the span of a moment I can usually manage cravings, exercise, doubts, worries, arguments, guilt, a sputtering self-image, and a crisis of faith.

A case in point: One night, Tom and I sparred over Wolfie and his girlfriend. He was on tour and still blinded by Liv. Most of our conversations were about his desire to visit her or arrange for her to visit him. I laughed off his social activity of long-distance play dates, but Tom thought I was too lenient and not paying enough attention. He thought I was setting Wolfie up for trouble by not cautioning him to slow down. He also worried that I paid more attention to his travel bills than the possibility he might make me a grandma ten years before I was ready.

I leaned back on the sofa and shook my head in quiet amazement at the way the two of us had changed sides in this matter. We hadn't articulated it quite this clearly before, but it was pretty apparent that at some point I had given up worrying about where Wolfie was sleeping and what might happen if, yikes, something unplanned happened.

To be honest, I had made sure Wolfie was informed. He knew I didn't want him to be a parent anytime soon, at least not until he learned to keep his bedroom clean (that's a joke, said nervously). I felt like I couldn't do anything else. I knew how I had been at his age. I didn't want to worry myself into five unwanted pounds.

In the meantime, Tom, who had no concerns about weight gain, worried freely and openly. He only seemed to think about condoms and unwanted pregnancies.

"It's because I have two daughters and you have one son," he said. "I worry about a million penises, and you just worry about one."

"Apparently not enough for you," I said.

"I'm just saying," he scoffed.

"And I'm just saying I can't worry about what I can't control," I explained. "It's like my age. I am getting older. I can't do anything about it. Instead of worrying, I'm planning the party I want when I turn fifty."

"Oh?" Tom asked.

"Think Italy."

"But what about Wolfie?"

"He can come if he's not at home taking care of my grandchild."

"Seriously."

"I am serious," I said. "Like I said, I don't have any way of controlling him. So I'm hoping that he won't get anyone pregnant. I'm hoping he will be responsible. I'm hoping that if he gets married it will work out. I'm hoping that if he gets his heart broken, it won't last too long. I'm hoping that all of his good qualities only get better when he's an adult. I'm hoping and praying that things work out. And for some reason, I think they will."

About a week later, Tom and I hit New York City for my birthday. We arrived from Cincinnati, where I had stopped for a book signing, and checked into our hotel. I woke up the next day to a happy-birthday kiss. After a workout in the hotel gym, I taped a segment on the *Rachael Ray* show. My parents surprised me by flying in and joining us for dinner at an Italian restaurant (big surprise), where we ordered my favorite champagne and clinked glasses.

"The only thing that bugs me about my age is that my knees ache when I get out of bed in the morning," I said.

"Then you get to be my age and you're delighted to be able to get out of bed in the morning," my mom cracked.

I asked my mom how old she was.

"Thirty-nine," she said.

"Good, that makes me about twelve," I said.

We reminisced about my previous birthdays. For my sixteenth, my mom got me a cake with pink elephant candleholders that I thought were cool. My eighteenth birthday had been a surprise party. I got married less than two weeks before my twenty-first birthday and spent my actual birthday ignoring the voice in my head that asked, "What the hell did you just do?"

At thirty, I was pregnant with Wolfie. Then I celebrated my fortieth with an all-girls party in Las Vegas, my least favorite city. But my marriage was winding down and I wanted to have some fun. I drove there in my new convertible, my "oh-my-God-I'm-forty car," as I called it. I'd bought it to satisfy a desire for more options in my life. I needed a change. I didn't find it in that car. It took a few more years to find those new options for change.

We were talking about cars when the waiter brought our starters. I ate half of my yummy pasta, then gave the rest to Tom. Within seconds, the waiter returned to the table to ask if everything was all right with my dish, offering to bring me another if I didn't like it. I explained that the pasta had been heavenly, but those few bites were all I needed.

I couldn't believe those words came from me. But I had a different outlook these days, whether talking about age or pappardelle alla buttera. For the most part, I took what I needed, not all that I wanted—except at the end of the meal when the waiter came to the table with a birthday cake. As I told everybody, not only did I need a slice of cake, I *wanted* a big one.

Notes to Myself

Someone, obviously not a fan, said, "Hey, wake up. It's not all about food." I was, like, Duh, but no one told me until I was forty-eight years old.

If I had to be reincarnated as food, I would choose Swiss cheese. It's the holiest.

One more thing to remember. Change comes from the inside. It's often the last thing you're going to see when you look in the mirror. So be patient.

Chapter Nine

The Clean Spot on the Ceiling

The next time Tom and I were in New York City, I was already sick when we landed at the airport. I got even sicker as we drove into the city and went straight to the hotel, where I thought about crawling into bed but instead realized I had fifteen minutes to freshen up and go attend a lunch for UNICEF at Michael's, a star-packed restaurant where the beautiful people dined while I coughed into my napkin for ninety minutes.

"Are you going to see a doctor?" someone at the table asked.

"No, I'm fine," I said. "It'll clear up."

The following afternoon I taped a segment for Rachael Ray, and the next day *Ladies Home Journal* hosted a lunch in my honor. Around that time, something had happened in the ongoing saga about New York Attorney General Elliot Spitzer, and everyone was talking about the latest development, including me. Between coughs and sneezes, I offered an opinion to anyone who would listen. At one point, I sneezed right on columnist Michael Musto.

"You should see a doctor," a publicist said.

"I'm okay," I said, wiping my nose.

I really wasn't. I knew the best thing to do whenever I begin to feel run down or sick is to stop for a couple of days and rest. But I didn't have time—or so I told myself.

My body didn't care about my appointment book, though. After dinner, we went back to the hotel and I took a bath to see if I could steam some of the crud out of me. I came out of the bathroom and told Tom it hadn't worked and he should probably call a doctor. He was ecstatic. He had been urging me to see a doctor for a week or more, long before we left L.A.; and as much as he hated to see me sick, he loved feeling like he had been right all along.

I swear, he was almost gloating as he dialed the doctor recommended by the hotel's concierge.

"Take the smile off your face," I said.

"I'm just saying," he muttered, turning away so I couldn't see him.

Following a brief examination, the doctor pronounced me sick. I raised an eyebrow at him, as if to say, "Oh really?" He said I had a chest infection and wrote me a prescription for antibiotics and cough medicine, which a nearby twenty-four hour pharmacy delivered to the hotel.

True confession: I happened to take too much cough medicine that night and in the morning, and codeine and I don't mix. Later that morning, I had to do a book signing and I arrived a little dizzy. By the next day, though, I was at a Costco in New Jersey, doing another book signing, and I felt much better. I think it was the comfort of being surrounded by two of my passions, literature and food.

We ended up staying through the weekend, and by Sunday morning I felt back to myself. As always after recovering from a bout of something, I was incredibly grateful to have my health back. Tom and I went out for breakfast and took a walk afterward. It was a gorgeous day. The air was crisp and fresh, and that and the energy of the city itself brought me fully back to life.

It was the kind of day when I really love New York. The streets were coming alive. The sidewalks were filled with the delicious smells of food carts, including sizzling sausages and chicken kabobs on the grill. I saw a guy chomp down on a hot dog teeming with sauerkraut even though it was not yet noon. I envied him living on the edge like that—ha!

Tom and I walked past storefronts and down streets until we had gotten lost—lost in the way that the activity itself overtook us and we forgot our original destination, if we even had had one. But to paraphrase the writer Douglas Adams: you may set out for one place but you end up where you need to be. And so it was with us.

Tom needed a restroom. We walked a couple of blocks until we found a friendly store, Saks Fifth Avenue.

"Let's go inside," I said. "I'll go to the makeup counter and have some fun."

I did exactly that and was paying for some YSL cosmetics when Tom found me again. I gave him a look that said, "Don't worry. I'm done. You aren't going to have to wait around while I shop. We can leave."

We went outside and debated which way to turn. We thought we might stroll through Central Park, a change of pace from the brisk walks we usually take through the lovely acreage whenever we visit. We headed north but only got about a half block before stopping in front of St. Patrick's Cathedral. We stared up at the neo-gothic towers, its nearly 160-year-old spires rising the length of a football field. I put my arm through Tom's and said, "It's freaking gorgeous, isn't it?"

In all the times I had been to New York over the years, I had walked past the church a thousand times and never paused to admire its beauty. Tom suggested we go inside.

"I think it's closed," I said.

"But look, people are going in and out," he said. "Let's check it out."

We walked up the stairs and went inside. I was wrong; it wasn't closed. In fact, it was very much open for business. We were only a few steps in when we heard someone whisper that Mass was starting in five minutes. We looked at each other and decided to stay. We walked down the side aisle and took a seat near the front. We didn't have a view of the priest or anything else going on in front, but that was all right with me. I was there for the ambiance—or so I said.

As I told Tom, I hadn't been in a Catholic church for Mass since I'd taken part in my first Holy Communion in Delaware when I was seven years old. My mother sewed a beautiful dress for me that looked like a little white wedding gown. After putting it on, I felt so pretty that I wanted to wear it all the time.

Unlike me, Tom had grown up going to church every Sunday, and he continued through most of his adulthood. From the time we met, we talked about the Bible and God and spirituality in general. It was the first time that my life included the idea of faith and trust in God's bigger picture, and I liked it. I didn't all of a sudden embrace religion, but I felt a curiosity. It was kind of like having foie gras for the first time. I enjoyed the taste, but I didn't have it every day. Yet the next time I encountered it, I had another enjoyable taste.

Over time and through talks with Tom, I came to realize that I always had believed in God. But Tom and I had very different relationships with God. He accepted God without question. His belief had been cemented in childhood, and that feeling had not wavered through adulthood, even when he experienced some pretty tumultuous times. As he told me, that's when he trusted God the most.

By contrast, I was filled with questions. I was one of those who said, "I believe in God, but . . ." Several times during my darkest years, I had gone looking for a spiritual connection, some sort of deeper understanding of a master plan that would enable me to make sense of my pain and misery. I went to church. I dabbled in Kabbalah. I meditated at the Self-Realization Fellowship. All of them offered something, but none of them felt completely right to me.

People have religious experiences in countless ways and places, from seeing the Virgin Mary on a moldy piece of bread to gazing at the world from the top of a mountain. Besides my grandmother's soup, only one other thing had made a lasting impression on me as real and genuine and truly holy. The wafer I had tasted during communion when I was seven years old. It had been delicious.

"I can still remember the taste," I told Tom. "Like the outside part of a *torrone* or nougat candy."

"What is it with you?" he asked. "You remember your grandma's soup and a wafer."

"I don't know," I said, shrugging. "Maybe subconsciously I have always thought eating would get me closer to God."

Hey, I wouldn't have been the first Italian to think of a good meal as a spiritual experience. Maybe that's why my search for God had been so frustrating. I'd wanted a tangible, show-me type of spiritual moment that would let me *get it*. I'd wanted to see it, feel it, hold it, and taste it, like a life-changing meatball.

As we sat in St. Patrick's, I glanced around the vast room and soaked up the serene atmosphere, marveling at the contrast between the hubbub outside on the street and the peace inside this sanctuary just several hundred yards away. Whether it was the Lord's presence or a holiness that people ascribed to this place, something undeniably spiritual was in the air.

I didn't follow the sermon as closely as Tom did. To me, it was like nice music playing; sometimes I listened, and sometimes I let it fade into the background while my mind drifted. I prayed for strength and guidance. I asked God to keep those I loved healthy. I asked for peace. And I requested a little bit of help watching over Wolfie since I had clearly slacked off.

At one point, I found myself thinking again about my grand-mother's cappelletti soup—not the actual soup as much as the feeling of warmth, comfort, peace, and okayness it inspired. I glanced over at Tom. His eyes were shut. He was communing with a higher power, and I was thinking of soup. I smiled. Maybe the two are different routes to the same place.

I was just glad to be on the path that would take me closer to God. Walking into St. Patrick's was a baby step on a long journey that could take the rest of my life, but I was glad to have at least taken the first one. I sensed it was an important part of maintenance—and it is.

From the time I had begun my diet, I'd had faith that I could lose weight. I didn't know where it came from, but I had it. Having reached my goal, I needed even more faith that I could keep it off.

Since maintenance was more complicated, I needed faith that I would find the strength and determination to meet the new challenges I faced. I needed faith that I was going in the right direction and would end up in a good and healthier place because, as I often say, I won't know if I've succeeded until the day I die.

Ultimately, I knew such faith has to come from me, from deep inside, like "the little engine that could" in the children's story, who said, "I think I can, I think I can. . . ." Maybe church was like a drive-through, one among many places where I could stop when I felt my soul craving nourishment.

One thing I knew for sure: I was still hungry—as hungry as I had ever been. It was a different kind of hunger, though: one that I couldn't satisfy with food—and had no desire to. It was the same yearning I had noticed in friends and other women around my age. All of us had reached a point where we had sought comfort or escape in food, drugs, alcohol, or shopping, learned they didn't work, and now found ourselves wanting something deeper and more genuine, something that would provide our lives with meaning and substance.

The priest was talking about a part of the Bible that didn't make sense to me. I couldn't tell if others were as lost as I was, though a discreet glance around made me think that most of them were paying better attention. Suddenly my stomach growled. It was a biggie, one of those loud gurgles that could be mistaken for old pipes rattling or a lion waking up. I guessed my stomach was still recovering from the night before. I looked around, hoping no one had heard, including Tom, who would have made a face asking what kind of monster was living inside me that I couldn't tame. But he didn't even flinch. He was scuba diving in the deep end of the

Holy Spirit. His eyes were closed, tears were sliding down his face, and he was praying to himself as if God were seated between us.

I stared at him in amazement. I wondered what the heck he had heard the priest say that I apparently had missed.

I would have been surprised but I wouldn't have complained, if this service had reshaped every one of my sixty-four-and-a-half inches, from the tippy top of my head to the ticklish bottom of my toes. I would have walked out of the church thinking it was meant to be. But nothing happened—not until the priest offered communion to anyone who wanted to accept the body of Christ.

All of a sudden I felt something inside me wake up—my stomach. I nudged Tom.

"I want to taste the cookie," I whispered.

"It's not a cookie," he said. "It's a wafer."

"Fine," I said. "I want to taste it."

"I don't know if you should."

"He said whoever wants it can go up there."

Tom took a deep breath. He didn't want to be embarrassed. He pointed out that you were only supposed to take communion if you had gone to confession. Neither of us had gone. I didn't care. We debated the issue. I argued that since we confessed our sins to each other every day, in voices easily audible to God, we were on safe ground.

"So you say," Tom said.

I fixed my eyes squarely and firmly on his. My jaw was clenched in that look he knew very well.

"I want the cookie," I said.

"Wafer," he corrected.

I looked toward the front, where people had lined up. Then I looked at Tom. It was double-dare-you time.

"I'll go if you go," he said.

I was already on my feet and walking toward the line. A few moments later, I accepted the wafer, then Tom did the same and we returned to our seats. Tom immediately saw the disappointment on my face. The wafer hadn't melted on my tongue like the one I remembered in Delaware. It tasted different. From what I could tell, I was the only one frowning at the taste of Christ.

I knew that my disappointment in the communion wafer didn't mean that I had any less love for Jesus than before. In fact, I may have had a little more affection for Him. But I was quite sure that if Jesus were alive and knew the variety of cookies available in your average grocery store, He would demand a better cookie be used than the tasteless wafer. A Nilla wafer at the least. But I could also envision Him wanting to treat his worshippers to double-stuffed Oreos, jam-filled pogens, or my mom's pizzelles.

As Tom lost himself again in prayer after we'd returned to our seats, I thought about using pizzelles instead of wafers. I imagined record crowds turning out for Mass if those pizzelles were cut up in little squares and served warm, with melted butter on top. I could see people skipping IHOP for church. Even better: Sara Lee coffee cake. I mean, put the two side by side, a wafer and coffee cake. Which would Jesus choose?

It dawned on me that my disappointment with the wafer was unreasonable. What had tasted good to me at seven wouldn't necessarily taste the same at forty-eight. Tastes, like nearly everything else in life, change. I figured the important thing was that the taste had stayed with me through all those years: vivid, pure, and sweet, the way that God might have reached out in an age-appropriate manner.

Now I had to find something else. I had to look around and be patient and open, mindful that God works on everyone, whether by providing a wonderful-tasting cookie, a beautiful piece of music, a hillside exploding with wild flowers, the unexpected kindness of a friend, or a challenging situation that makes you a better, stronger, and wiser person for having faced them. All of this defines maintenance—otherwise known as the rest of my life.

I was gazing at the stained glass windows as the service finally wound down to a solemn and (for Tom) satisfying conclusion. My eyes lingered on the shafts of light full of color as they entered the cathedral through the stained glass windows; I followed them upward to the ceiling, which was dirty—as if the smirches and sins that had been left in this church had collected up there like dirt in an air-conditioning filter. My eyes wandered across the ceiling until I saw one little patch that had been cleaned right above me. Compared to the rest of the ceiling, it sparkled. It was like a window. Inside that square, I thought I saw a flower. I stared at it until Tom put his arm around me and asked if that was my stomach growling.

"Are you hungry?" he asked.

I nodded.

Notes to Myself

✧

Grace never lasts long enough. But it's enough to keep you coming back for more.

I was wondering: if I stopped trying to please anyone other than myself, how would I dress, what would I eat, how would I spend my day, whom would I hang out with, how would I want to feel?

Hey, wrinkles and zits at almost fifty years of age. It's so not fair to be breaking out during T.T.O.M. But who said life would be fair?

Your inner voice is like a knock-knock joke. If you have to ask who's there, you don't get it. Back to work.

Chapter Ten

It's Not Fair

Tom and I were traveling again, this time to Chicago for the final two shows of Van Halen's North American tour. Wolfie had had a great if not life-changing time performing with the band. But I was ready to get my son back after nine months of letting him travel across the country with a bunch of veteran rockers.

Tom and I had his son Dominic with us on the plane. After the concerts, the two of them were going to visit Tom's parents in Ohio.

I looked at Dom and thought back to when Wolfie was ten years old. As much as I missed my son being that age, I was in a better place now than I was back then. I had come a long way since the start of the tour, too. Actually, both Wolfie and I had changed since that day before the tour started when I watched him walk out the front door and wave goodbye, promising me that he would be good and call regularly, while I worried whether I had packed him enough socks and underwear. Now he had a serious girlfriend, a business manager, and dozens of stories that let me know he had grown up.

Not that he was a paragon of maturity. A few weeks earlier, Wolfie had called from his Charlottesville hotel room to tell me that he and Matt were throwing fruit from a gift basket out the hotel room window.

"Why are you telling me this?" I'd asked.

"Ma, I want you to hear me having fun," he'd said.

Wonderful, I thought. He's trying to be like his father. I will be able to tell this story with such pride the next time I get together with the ladies in my book club and everyone boasts of their children's latest accomplishments.

But, in fact, he did give me reason to boast. A few days later, I received a call from Tom's seventy-nine-year-old mother, Helen, who had gone with Tom and other family members to see Van Halen in Cleveland. Other than a Seals & Crofts show in the 1970s, it was her first rock concert, and she wanted me to know that Wolfie had been a perfect host—"a very good boy," was how she put it—which was music to my ears.

What she didn't tell me was that she had stood right in front of Wolfie the entire show, all five-foot-two and 110 pounds of her, at the lip of the stage, screaming, "Hi, Wolfie! Hi, Wolfie!" He waved, threw her a guitar pick, and said, "Hi, Mrs. V." She kept screaming at him, "Hi, Wolfie." Finally, he knelt down—and mind you, this was during the show—and said, "Mrs. V, I can see you."

After landing in Chicago, Tom, Dominic, and I went straight to the hotel and met up with Wolfie, who asked if we liked our room. He was being sarcastic because I had insisted that Tom and I get one of the bedrooms in his two-bedroom suite. Apparently he was smarting over that. Ordinarily his road buddy, Matt, took the second bedroom. But I wanted family time while we were in town.

Wolfie was still asking what was wrong with a nice suite down the hall. I gave him credit. But I told him what was wrong. I was his mother.

"But that's not the way we usually do it," he said.

"I'm not usually on the road with you," I replied. "Don't worry. We'll make it fun."

He groaned that it wouldn't be like it was with Matt. I explained that it wasn't supposed to be. Trying to lighten the mood, I offered to walk around the suite in boxers if it helped. That just got me a dirty look. I eventually realized that I couldn't waltz in and impose myself just because I needed a fix of family time. Plus we weren't Wolfie's only visitors. He had also flown his girlfriend in for the final show, and he wanted to spend time alone with her, too.

"Where's Dom going to sleep?" he asked.

"On the fold-out sofa in front of your room," I chimed, much more casually than I had imagined delivering that news.

Wolfie thought about it for a second and then said, "Okay."

A few hours later, we were at the arena, all of us crammed into his dressing room. Wolfie showed incredible patience as I fussed with his hair, but he drew the line when I suggested all of us have a light dinner together and then play Euchre until the show. He explained that he had a pre-show routine. He also wanted to deal with an issue he was having with his bass. Then he took Liv's hand and they walked down the corridor, leaving Tom and me, the two old farts, with nothing to do but stare at each other as Dom and Alex Van Halen's son, Malcolm, played video games.

I shrugged apologetically. I'd forgotten that Wolfie had a job to do.

"Who allowed him to grow up?" I asked.

Tom put his arm around me and said, "You did, baby."

Later, we were still hanging out in Wolfie's dressing room when I noticed that the comfortable sofa that had been part of his dressing room setup on all the previous dates was no longer part of the décor. When I asked where it had gone, Wolfie gritted his teeth and said, "Dad and Janie took it."

"Hmm," I said.

"It's not fair," he said.

"Dude, it's not about fair," I said. "It's about your dad."

I noticed Liv give Wolfie a soothing love pat as I turned to Tom with my take on the relocated sofa. I interpreted it as a good thing, a sign that Janie was trying to get Ed to relax before shows, and therefore wanted the sofa in case he wanted to lie down or cozy up with her and talk. Maybe she was exerting more influence since their recent engagement. After putting the ring on her finger, Ed had come to my house and told me the news so I would know before reading it on the Internet.

As word spread, a couple of people asked me how I felt about the news. If they thought I would be upset, they didn't know me. I was happy for both Ed and Janie, a publicist who had survived numerous ups and downs with Ed. From what I had seen through-out the last year, she truly loved him. And Ed loved her.

These days, Ed appeared to be doing quite well. I saw him through Wolfie's open dressing room door. He had either recently arrived at the arena or just come out of his dressing room. He was pacing the hallway with his guitar, getting into the zone, that place he retreated to in order to get ready to perform.

Like many artists, Ed spent much of his time in his head. The youngest of two sons of Dutch musician Jan Van Halen and his wife, Eugenia, he was a music prodigy who played piano as a child and won numerous competitions. His parents had a volatile, sometimes violent marriage, and early on Ed escaped into his music. He learned the drums, but switched to guitar when his brother Alex showed more promise, and by his early teens he spent practically all of his waking hours practicing guitar—as he himself has said, sitting on the edge of his bed, his guitar slung over his shoulder, with tall cans of Schlitz malt beer and cigarettes nearby.

His life continued pretty much the same once he became an adult. Even as his bedrooms changed, stardom allowed him to stay in the comfort and familiarity of that dysfunctional bubble. In fact, he was rewarded for prolonging his adolescence—and, in my opinion, he suffered for it more than anyone acknowledged, including he himself.

When I thought back to Ed during our marriage, especially the first half, I pictured a sweet, sensitive, extraordinarily talented young man who, whether in the studio or with me, spent much of his energy battling demons. He seemed to continue battling them through the early part of this tour. I was happy to see him out in the hallway looking much better.

We were in some ways two peas from the same pod. He knew my imperfections, a long list of them, as well as anybody. The difference was I had worked on shedding my unhappiness and making my life healthier. I hoped it had made an impression on him, and maybe even inspired him in some way not only to get his shit together at age fifty-three but also to discover that he was a much better man than he let himself believe.

A short time later, I saw him in the hallway again, this time holding Janie's hand. He looked sweet. I hoped she could lead him to places I hadn't been able to. I also hoped he would let her.

Meanwhile, Wolfie and Liv returned to his dressing room. I sensed he wanted some alone time with her before the show. All of a sudden the room felt crowded, more so than when all four of us had shared it an hour earlier. Tom and I and the kids excused ourselves to take a walk. Basically, we'd been booted. Pretending to be upset, I took Tom's hand and grumbled, "It's not fair."

Laughing, he asked, "Where have I heard that before?"

During the show, Tom walked around with the little boys, Dominic and Malcolm. They ended up in front of the stage as Alex went into his drum solo. Tom hoisted Malcolm up on his shoulders so he could see his dad.

I was perched on the side of the stage in almost the same place I had stood when I was married to Ed. Only now, all these years later, I was on the other side of the stage, sharing the space with Wolfie's girlfriend, and enjoying how thoroughly happy both Wolfie and Ed looked playing with each other. I smiled. It was easy to forget how personal the music is to Ed, and it gave me a warm feeling to see the two of them sharing it.

As Alex continued to wail on the drums, Wolfie came over to visit me and Liv (or vice versa). He started to tell Liv something and I saw him get agitated. When I asked if something was wrong, he said some guy up front was "drunk off his ass" and distracting him.

"What's he doing?" I asked.

"He keeps flipping me off," Wolfie said.

My mother-hen instinct took over and I said, "I'll take care of it."

"No, mom!" he said. "Please! It's happened before. I'll get through it."

Sure he would. But I didn't know if I could.

"I just want to tell him to not be mean to you," I said.

"No you aren't," Wolfie said. "I know you. I can see the headline in the tabloids: 'Valerie Bertinelli Goes Apeshit at Van Halen Concert. Attacks Fan.' It will not look good."

"Okay, fine," I said, knowing what I was going to do anyway.

As soon as Wolfie went back onstage, I went back to my place out front and began looking for the guy. Sure enough, I saw some guy drunk off his ass, flipping him off. He was probably four people away from me. I made eye contact with his girlfriend, who nudged him. Suddenly, I was locking eyes with this a-hole. He began to grin, but I raised my right index finger and shook it at him. I shook the smile off his face, too. I'm sure Wolfie saw me from the stage. So did security, who took the guy away before I could get into it with him.

I rode back to the hotel with Wolfie, Liv, Tom, and Dominic. As they discussed the show, I gazed out the window and saw Ed and Janie's limo in the lane next to us and beyond them the twinkling bright lights of downtown Chicago. I was in a reflective mood, thinking about the long journey that had brought all of us to this point where everyone was in a good place—better in fact than we had been a year earlier.

As we sped along the freeway, I had no complaints. I wondered if this were a state of grace, a moment of answered prayer when God reached His hand down to me and said, "Hey, feel this. This is what I'm talking about. This is your cappelletti soup."

We woke up the next day to extraordinary weather. We had been invited to go out on Lake Michigan. The lovely man who owned the limousine service the band uses took all of us for a day-long cruise on his boat. Not expecting to need a bathing suit in Chicago, I picked up a pair of shorts and a tank top at the marina, something I never would have done a few years earlier. I would have suffered in long pants and a long-sleeved shirt.

As we motored around the lake, I saw a water ski line and inner tube in the back of the boat and suggested we try it. Wolfie and I were the only ones who were game. He wanted to go first. He climbed down onto the back and stuck his leg in the water. It was ice cold. He immediately hoisted himself back on deck and said, "No way."

A moment later, I jumped down, grabbed the inner tube, stuck my butt in the center and flew backwards into the chilly blue water. Tom let out a whoop and I heard Wolfie shout, "Mom, you are crazy!"

Notes to Myself

⁕

It's nice to get home and feel more comfortable than I do in the fanciest hotels.

The woman giving me a pedicure was talking to another woman in a language I didn't understand, and like every woman I got paranoid they were talking about me. What would be worse—if they said I was fat? Or if I have ugly toes? (which I don't).

As long as I'm obsessing about feet, I have decided that getting a foot massage is as important as letting God into your life. One deals with your sole, the other with your soul. But both are integral to a strong foundation.

Rule of thumb: stop over-thinking and just get on with what's right.

Chapter Eleven

Checking the Mail

Three days after the Van Halen show in Chicago, Tom and I were walking along Michigan Avenue when a woman stopped us and thanked me for inspiring her to lose weight. From the sunny nature of our brief exchange, which included taking a photo with her, it was impossible to tell that I was having a bad day. But inside my head, a voice said, "Me, an inspiration? Clearly, you have the wrong person."

Some days I didn't feel that I was either a size inspiration or a size perfect, and this was one of those days. The night before, I had learned there wasn't any room for me on the private jet taking Wolfie, Ed, Dave, and Al, as well as their significant others, to Grand Rapids, the last gig of the tour. Seeing the final shows, including the very last one, was the reason I had come out in the first place. I took the news personally—and probably too emotionally.

I shouldn't have been as upset as I was. I can't even count how many Van Halen shows I have seen since I first met Ed at a show in 1980. I have followed the band for twenty-eight years, and not always because I wanted to. It was like they say in *The Godfather*: "just when you think you're out, they pull you back in." Now I was back in, but my son didn't always want me around as much as I wanted to be around. . . . I don't know. I was conflicted and confused.

Anyway, I was pissed. I took the lack of a seat as a personal slight, and it wasn't. There just wasn't a seat.

Then at the last minute, I received word of an extra seat on the plane. By then, I was in too foul a mood and said no thanks.

Was I over-reacting? Yes. I couldn't help it. Family is my top priority, and I felt like I was being denied access to an important event in my son's life. All sorts of emotions boiled to the surface. The outburst was unlike me. I warned Tom to keep his distance. Normally I am fairly even-tempered and maybe guilty of not caring enough about certain things, but I was tired and cranky from too much travel and the pressure of having to be "on" and upbeat way more than normal.

At lunch, I shoveled food in me until Tom asked if I thought I might be eating my anger. If he had just made a comment, I probably would have snapped at him. But since he had asked a question, I had no choice but to stop and consider whether I had lapsed back into that dark place I thought I had left way behind. The answer was clear: yes, I had—and it shocked my eyes wide open.

I put down my fork and asked the waiter to clear my plate and the evil basket of bread in front of me. I regrouped with Tom by talking out my frustrations. I was aware of what had happened. My feelings had sailed out of control. I had gone from being upset about being denied a seat on a plane, to asking whether Wolfie appreciated my efforts to be with him, to wondering whether or not I was a good mother. In reality, I was simply hurt and had handled it poorly.

I was most disturbed by how easily feelings of inadequacy and self-doubt got back in my head, and also how quickly I had returned to bad habits. It was the definition of my old bugaboos, unconscious behavior, and emotional eating. It was also a wake-up that progress—in my case, maintenance—happens in fits and starts. I wasn't going to be perfect every day.

"It's not fair," I groused to Tom. "If I don't want to regain the weight I've lost, but if I want to keep trying to be the best me, I have to be vigilant every day for the rest of my life."

"Yup," he said.

"Who wants to be vigilant every frickin' day forever?"

I calmed down and began to think in terms of a more manageable time frame than forever. Ah-ha! So that's what was meant by living in the moment. I could handle a moment; forever was too much. With twenty-four hours to kill, Tom and I worked out and saw the city. In the afternoon, Wolfie called from the venue to say they had finished the sound check and he felt good about that night's show. That night, he called again to say the show had gone well and they were back on the plane, heading back to Chicago.

"Love you," he said before hanging up.

"Love you, too."

Wolfie and I flew home the next day while Tom and his son went to Ohio. I was still out of sorts, and feeling pressured. I had two days to settle Wolfie back home after he'd been three-quarters of a year on the road; then I planned to fly to Ohio for a weekend of long-planned parties for Tom's family, including his parents' sixtieth wedding anniversary. It was too much to do in too little time.

I felt stretched too thin. It was the first time I had felt anything in my life was too thin.

Wolfie was bugging me, too. He rattled off all the things he wanted to do now that he was going to be home for a long stretch. They included taking advantage of his driver's license, hanging out with his friend Zack, and indulging in his love of gadgetry at the Apple store. In my state, I was sensitive to what I felt was a glaring omission on his list—spending time with me.

I had imagined that we would spend a day together getting resettled and talking about this amazing experience he'd had touring with Van Halen, seeing the country, being away from home, and in many ways growing up. But I realized that was my fantasy and perhaps I needed to process the past year more than he did. As it turned out, we spent the first full day back home together, anyway. I took him to meet his new business manager, and on the way back home we ran a few errands.

For a few moments, including the one when we walked across the grocery store parking lot, we were back to our old selves, Wolfie and his mom, two inseparable compadres spending all their time together. Back home, the illusion ended. Word had spread among Wolfie's friends that he was back and the phone rang nonstop, as did his cell phone. And on the few occasions I saw him pass through a room, he was texting.

Several times, I called out, "Hey, what's up?" In return, I got a "Love you, Mom." One time, he actually paused and asked me for advice. He wanted to know where he should go to get Liv a necklace. Meanwhile, Tom's son, Tony, was preparing for his senior prom. He needed help renting a tux, picking a corsage, and organizing a group of friends who would share expenses on a limo.

Those two days were hectic. By the time I got on the plane to Ohio, I felt that I hadn't accomplished one thing. I sat there thinking that even though I had done the "lighten" part of enlightenment, I didn't know how to pull it all together. For much of the flight, I pressed my nose out the window and scanned the clouds for signs of God. I would have settled for a UFO. But Cleveland came up before either one.

Tom and his parents picked me up at the airport. On the way to the hotel, they gave us the low-down on the relatives who had come into town for the three celebrations: Tom's sister Angela's son's high school graduation, his cousin Pat's fiftieth birthday, and their own sixtieth anniversary. Mention of each party included a description of the food. It sounded more like a three-day Italian food festival.

Suddenly I felt the urge to exercise. If my calculations were right, I would have to walk back to Los Angeles to burn off all the calories I would likely consume. It might have been the after-effects of my breakdown in Chicago, but I was seriously worried about being able to resist what seemed to me the perfect storm of temptation. Mortadella, lasagna, and biscotti—I had to remind myself that these were not my friends. I also had to remind myself, in a voice that sounded a little like Forrest Gump's mother, that "Jenny Craig always said there'd be days like these."

As I feared, the test began that night with a casual dinner— several pepperoni-and-cheese pizzas. I smelled them coming through the front door as they arrived from the local pizzeria.

"I suspect that's what Heaven smells like," I said to Tom.

"Or Hell," he said.

I shrugged.

"Whichever one it is, I'm going there if it smells that good."

To my credit, I managed not to over-eat. My secret? I talked nonstop. Between Tom's mother, sister, aunts, and cousins, I found myself amid a compassionate and sympathetic sisterhood who sensed I was off, drew me out of my shell, listened to my complaints, and assured me that I wasn't a loser. All of them said they had been through the same thing with their children that I was going through with Wolfie.

Tom's sister reminded me of the old adage that, if you want to make God laugh, make plans. Then she added, "If you want to feel unappreciated and taken for granted, try to do something nice for your kids."

"That's me," I said, raising my hand in acknowledgment.

"We don't notice it as much when they're little," she said. "They're too cute. We forgive them too quickly."

"Yeah."

"But then they become teenagers. . . ."

I was fully aware of the possibility that I, like many other mothers I knew, might be needier than I realized. My expectations for hugs and thank you's might have been based on memories from when my child wanted to hang on my leg and look up at me as if I were the Statue of Liberty. As I was learning in other areas of my life, I had to recognize changes around me, adapt to them, and change myself and my own reactions. Like when I called home the next morning to check in on Wolfie and hear how Tony's prom had gone.

Wolfie answered, and I could tell that I had woken him up. After extracting a few key details—Wolfie was fine, Tony had gotten back late, a few people had forgotten to pay him for the limo and he was still asleep—I let Wolfie go back to sleep. He promised to call me later. Before hanging up, he said, "Love you."

That night, Angela threw a party for her son's high school graduation. We arrived en masse: Tom; his two daughters, who had flown in from Arizona; his younger son; and me. We hugged and kissed everyone hello and then walked straight into a spread of impossibly delicious food. It started with a platter of assorted olives, cheeses, and breads and ended with iced Italian twist cookies that Tom's Aunt Syl had baked earlier in the day. I only got as far as the warm potato salad, made with bacon and cheese, by the way, before groaning that I half expected to hear someone shout, "Dead man walking."

I didn't want to harp on the food, but, my God, there was so much of it—and this was just the start of the celebrations. Nonetheless, I managed to pace myself and exercise incredible self-control.

Later that night, I did some soul-searching about what I could reasonably expect from myself in such situations. Though I didn't want to fall off my diet, I also wanted to be able to enjoy myself and not miss out on life's special occasions. I didn't want to walk into every party or event full of worry and leave full of guilt.

I realize that the keys to maintenance are balance and moderation, but I also know that people have struggled with those concepts since the dawn of time—no doubt since the first meal where dessert was served and someone asked for a second helping. Why would I find it any easier?

I didn't, and the next morning I struggled to get ready for Mr. and Mrs. Vitale's sixtieth wedding anniversary. I had packed five outfits for three days, tried on every one of them, and didn't feel comfortable in anything. Then I tried to mix and match. Nothing was right. Standing stark naked, I turned to Tom and announced that I couldn't find a thing to wear.

"Nothing feels right," I said.

He looked at me with eyes as wide as two-lane tunnels.

"Come here and let me feel," he said.

"Shut up," I snapped. "You don't understand. Nothing's working."

"You don't understand," he replied. "I'm looking at you and everything's working for me."

I appreciated his support even though it got him nowhere. Finally, I gave up on feeling comfortable and put on nice jeans and a top I had tried on forty-five minutes earlier, the outfit I had originally planned to wear. We drove to Thistledown Race Track, where Tom's family had reserved a private room for an afternoon of eating and betting on the horses. From the looks of the buffet table, I thought the smart money should be put on the chicken marsala and the lasagna.

Unfortunately, I just wasn't in the mood for visiting and found a perch off in the corner and watched the room fill up with Tom's family and friends. I listened to the rounds of toasts and congratulations, wondering why I couldn't shake my crappy mood during such a relaxed, joyous, loving, and festive event.

Tom was patient. He gave me time and space and then finally came over and dragged me out of the corner. It was as if he sensed I needed to be pulled away from myself. He was right. Soon I was immersed in a conversation with Angela about her parents' marriage. I was curious what she thought they had done right that enabled them to stay married for more than a half century.

"Tenacity," she said.

"It has to be more than that," I said.

"Not only did my parents' generation stay together, I don't think they expected everything to be perfect or problem-free," said Angela, who described her parents' values as old-fashioned and out of step with those today. "They thought about family first and measured success in ways that were much different than nowadays."

I knew what she meant. They weren't consumed with partying and playing like they were in their twenties when they were in their fifties. They didn't think about staying young forever. They didn't spend every day focused on their own selves. They didn't worry about keeping up with the latest fashions because the things they valued never went out of fashion.

What Angela was talking about, and what I agreed with, was a sense of being real. I obviously don't believe in staying in a marriage that is miserable for one or both of the parties. I don't believe in staying together just for the kids, either, though for children to have two parents who love each other is preferable to having only one parent in their lives. On the other hand, having one loving parent is better than having two parents who are hateful.

But Angela described her parents in ways that sounded an awful lot like mine. At their core are simple values that I admire, like honesty, trust, hard work, love, and a sense, as Tom has said, of busting your ass to get the most out of life.

Mr. Vitale had retired from B.F. Goodrich, where he made tires for forty-two years. Every few years he had been laid off or the union had gone on strike, Angela remembered, but he was willing to do any sort of work to provide for his family. He usually worked as a butcher; in fact, he often did that at night in addition to his day job. Plus he was an astute investor, a skill he taught himself, which enabled the family to live comfortably beyond his factory-worker salary.

Mrs. Vitale stayed at home and cared for her five children, her top priority. Angela recalled coming home from school and being greeted first by the thick, wonderful smells of pasta sauce simmering on the stove, and then by her mother.

"She canned her own tomatoes and made her own jam," she said. "She even made her own potato chips."

My mouth watered.

"And the house was always spotless," she said. "The woman is phenomenal. We thought everyone lived that way."

They weren't perfect, she emphasized. They had gone through their share of ups and downs as a couple. But they had maintained their commitment to family and that always seemed to be enough to renew their commitment to each other. They shared a feeling of responsibility, she said. And they never worried during lean times because they had always given to other people, always found time to extend a helping hand or show up with a meal, and they were confident that that would come back to them if they hit a rough patch.

"My dad never walked past anyone," she said. "Whether it was money, time, or something else, he gave."

"Amazing," I said.

"What's truly amazing?" she said "They always felt blessed."

Although I was grateful for Angela's company and conversation, all the talking about the importance of family made me feel guilty for not being home with Wolfie. My primary job was being his mother, yet I was two thousand miles away with Tom's family. The disappointment I felt in myself brought one unexpected realization. In trying to satisfy everyone, I may have been failing myself.

As soon as it was convenient, I checked in with Wolfie. I got his voicemail and left a message. I asked if he had taken enough pictures of Tony's prom, which I had asked him to do. A little while later he texted me back: "At Dad's. Took pix. Having fun. Don't worry."

Early the next morning, Tom and I met Angela for breakfast. I was feeling guilty about not being home; Tom was, too. I hated being out of sync and opened up a bit to Angela, who listened like an older sister and recalled how she had gone through a rough patch herself a few years earlier. In telling the story, she said something that really piqued my interest. She said that she had felt as if God had abandoned her in a time of need.

She got angry all over again as she remembered getting out of bed one night and driving to her church, looking for someone with whom she could speak, and hoping to commune with God in His house. But the door was locked.

"I was, like, you've got to be kidding me," she said. "I cried all the way home."

"What did you do?" I asked.

"I went to bed and I prayed this really nasty prayer," she said. "It was more like a challenge. All my life I'd been told that God would be there for me when I needed Him. In fact, I was told, He was there all the time. Then I went to His House and I couldn't get in. What was that about? And so I said, I need to believe in you more than ever. So let me know if you are there. Or else."

"Or else what?" I asked.

"It was going to be or else I need to re-evaluate," she said. "As it turned out, I woke up in the morning and went, 'Oh, my gosh.' I was different. And I've been different ever since."

"Different?" I asked. "How so?"

"I went to bed thinking I wasn't loved," she said. "I woke up knowing that wasn't true."

"Just like that?" I asked.

"Just like that."

I thought, B.S. I was too cynical right then to think that God would enter my life with the suddenness of a light switching on. For the past week or so, I had been going through my own mini-crisis of faith. After months of successful maintenance, I wasn't feeling great about myself. This trip and the previous one to Chicago had brought that into focus. I had been trying to figure out what had changed, what might be missing, if I was coasting or doing something wrong.

I had tried listening to my inner voice, but it wasn't talking to me. Or if it was, I couldn't hear it. Unlike Angela, I didn't think answers came overnight. I was wrong.

A few days after we returned home, I went out to get the mail and got set to toss out the stuff I consider junk when something in the stack caught my eye. I pulled out the piece of paper and found myself staring at text from I Corinthians 13:4–7:

> Love is patient, love is kind.
> It does not envy, it does not boast.
> It is not proud.
> It is not rude, it is not self-seeking, it is not easily angered.
> It keeps no record of wrongs.
> Love does not delight in evil but rejoices with the truth.
> It always protects, always trusts, always hopes, always perseveres.

I read it several times, looking for an advertisement from a church or a charity, a shelter or someplace. I couldn't find anything. It was just the message printed on a piece of paper with a lovely graphic of a flower. It was a beautiful thing to get in the mail and to think about as I went on with my day, which was what I did.

I set the paper on the counter with the rest of the mail. Later on, after I read through the mail, I stuck the paper in the fruit bowl. I found it again that night as I cleaned up from dinner. For the next few days, the paper seemed to follow me around the house. I would read it, move it, rediscover it, re-read it, and so on. Several days went by before I remembered to show Tom, who immediately remembered our talk with Angela and asked if I thought it might be a sign.

"Could be," I said with a shrug. "Anything could be. If I struggle to open a bag of chips, I take that as a sign from God that I'm not supposed to have them. It depends how much you're willing to read into something."

Tom didn't like my response. So I quickly added that it was a wonderful message to receive for no apparent reason.

A few days later, without any explanation, I woke up feeling differently about the paper. I don't even know why it popped into my head. It struck me as funny the way that sometimes happens. It might have been because somehow it got wet when one of the boys was doing the dishes, and I put it on the counter to dry in the sun. I already knew the obvious, namely that God wasn't going to help in the countless tasks I had to do and decisions I had to make every day to stay the course that would produce the best me. That was up to me.

On the other hand, He was just going to love me as much as I wanted and as much as I needed and as much as I let Him—even on those days I didn't love myself.

Notes to Myself

✀

Didn't sleep well after catching the boys in a lie. What they lied about wasn't as important as the message we tried to get across, and that is this: Tell the truth. It's easier to remember.

I made asparagus last night for dinner, and I swear it was one of the most delicious things I've ever eaten—and so easy: clean the asparagus, set on a cookie sheet, drizzle with olive oil and Kosher salt, roast at 425 degrees for six to eight minutes.

But why does asparagus make your pee smell? It turns out no one knows for sure. It only happens to about 40 to 50 percent of those who eat it, including me.

Wolfie pleaded with me not to mention the thing about beets.

Chapter Twelve

Continuing Education

As far as the choreography went, it was simple: one step up, glance down at the number, then step off, turn, and smile. The moves were so practiced, precise, and quick, I could have been performing a dance. Instead, I was weighing myself. But there was a slight change this time. The smile that was usually there at the end was replaced by a frown. Make that a grimace.

"What the . . . ? "

After more than a year of the numbers going down or staying the same when I stepped on the scale, I was shocked to see them take a turn in the opposite, and wrong, direction. We were just back from Ohio, where I knew that I had eaten more than I should have, and the things I had eaten belonged to a food group best described as Italian. Which meant too much cream sauce, cheese, butter, and starch.

No one would have blamed me if I had panicked, but I stayed

calm and kept my wits about me. I told Tom that I had just had my "Holy shit" moment, my long-awaited and feared reminder that I wasn't immune to any of the slips and setbacks that plagued millions of other people on maintenance and on diets. I talked it through with Tom, who was a wonderfully patient listener. Just because the numbers had gone up this one time didn't mean I had fallen off track permanently or even temporarily. No, it meant that I had partied a little too hard over one long weekend and I had to get back on the program.

It also meant that I had to accept that even though I had been a size fantastic for months, I wasn't perfect. I was as fallible as anyone else. I felt like this backslide was inevitable. Things had been good for too long. In the back of my head, I had been waiting for the other shoe to drop.

Tom frowned at that theory. He suggested taking responsibility for simply having eaten too much, as he had done, too. He was right. The mistake I had made when I'd been on previous diets was to let one bad day turn into two or three, then set a date the following week when I would put a stake in the ground and turn things around again. If I were to do that, though, before I knew it, I'd have been 10 or 15 pounds heavier, depressed, and in a bad frame of mind that really would have turned into a self-fulfilling prophecy of gaining more weight.

Now, I knew better, and the stakes were too high. It wasn't just the threat of public humiliation if I gained back my weight. It was the disappointment I would feel in myself. I called Kathy, my personal consultant, and told her what was going on. I also got back on a strict eating and exercise regimen. And I slowed down. I cancelled all but the most essential meetings: I regrouped and reprioritized.

Within a week, my weight was back where I wanted it. I realized that I do have the tools to keep myself from falling back into the dark, self-destructive behavior that had been the ruin of so many diets. I didn't get depressed or binge. I felt like I came to terms with the frailties and fallibilities of being human. It didn't make me any less good than before. It just made me wake up and see me.

The timing couldn't have been better. With Wolfie done with the tour and all of my serious travel finished, I was able to finally stay home. Mornings began at the kitchen table without an agenda, without cameras or microphones in my face, without anything to do but enjoy my cup of coffee, the crossword puzzle, and my cat Dexter lying nearby. It wasn't necessarily quiet, though. Issues arose. I spoke to Wolfie about his spending, and in a lecture that would be familiar to many parents, told him that a credit card was not a free pass.

Then there was my house itself. The numerous places that had been in serious need of repair six months earlier still needed to be repaired.

And finally there was me. While my managers, Jack and Marc, fielded offers and sorted the good from the bad as well as the viable from the waste of time, I took a long look in the mirror. I had spent months talking to the press about what I had done to lose 40 pounds. But I sensed I hadn't spent enough time figuring out what else I needed to do to keep evolving.

My brief setback had been more than a warning sign about my eating habits. It had also reminded me that I needed to continue dealing with a lifetime of insecurity and self-doubt, feelings that I was "less than" and undeserving of all the fortunate things that had happened to me. Those were the creepy crawlers that could undermine the hard work, denial, and self-discipline that had produced all the changes I was proud of. I was at a crossroads that many women know but few talk about: after working up the courage to make a profound life change, then mustering the faith and determination to accomplish it, I had to decide whether I believed that I deserved this slimmer, smarter, healthier version of myself, especially in the wake of slips and setbacks.

I thought it was important to keep moving forward by addressing the roots of those insecurities. For me, one was education. I had always been self-conscious about not having my high school diploma or a college degree. "I've always felt behind everyone else," I told a reporter for *People* magazine in the mid '90s. More than ten years after that admission, I didn't feel that I had gained any ground.

In an effort to correct that deficiency, I decided to get my GED and maybe take courses beyond high school. As a first step, I sent for my high school transcripts. As far as I could recall, I had left school only two credits shy of getting my diploma. However, after my transcripts arrived, I discovered I needed an entire semester of classes. How could I have made such a big mistake?

Then again, I had apparently taken a half semester of French. Not only could I not remember how to conjugate a single verb, I couldn't remember ever taking the class. On the other hand, I did remember taking advanced composition, U.S. government, and drama. My grades were a smattering of A's and B's, with one C in typing, which I remember rationalizing at the time as inconsequential since I was going to be an actress. Judging from my transcript, though, my drama teacher disagreed. She had given me a B in advanced drama.

"Look at that!" I exclaimed while showing the transcript to Tom. "What was that about? Is it too late to go back and argue the grade?"

Going back didn't interest me as much as moving forward. With the presidential campaign on the news every night, everyone seemed to have cast eyes on the future. I was swept up in Obama's talk of change. He supplied a fresh breath of hope, something I thought we needed, as distressing news increased about a faltering economy and plummeting trust in government, businesses, leaders, CEOs, and other pillars that were supposed to make our country great.

People can get by on a lot less than they think; but they need hope. Experience had taught me that hope comes from doing hard work, facing hard truths, correcting past mistakes, making your own breaks, taking risks, daring yourself to grow, and seeing the progress.

It doesn't always work out as planned. Ages ago, back when I was pregnant, during another quest to make up for my lack of formal education, I had purchased a set of leather-bound novels, The 100 Greatest Books Ever Written. I had every intention of reading them. I imagined how smart and satisfied I would feel after completing all 100. But after nearly twenty years, I have only read one, *Pride and Prejudice*. Or was it *Sense and Sensibility*? Oh, brother.

Despite that other false start, I was enthusiastic about my new plan for completing my education. As a reminder, I left my transcript in plain view on the dining room table where I kept all my important paperwork and investigated courses. I sent for a catalog from a nearby community college. What could be more inspiring than reading through a catalog of college courses? I sat up in bed at night, paging through the classes and elbowing Tom every time I found a course that sounded great. I was especially interested in religious studies and art history.

"I would love to have been in the studio when Leonardo da Vinci was painting Mona Lisa. I'd love to know what they were talking about as he worked. And how long it took him to paint that picture."

"You don't have to take a class," said Tom. "You can look up that information now if you really want to."

Eventually I sat down at the computer and looked up da Vinci's masterpiece on Wikipedia. I was fascinated. His subject was believed to be Lisa del Giocondo, the wife of wealthy Florentine merchant, Francesco del Giocondo, who commissioned the painting in honor of the birth of their second son, Andrea, although the subject's actual identity was debated for centuries. Apparently the painting itself didn't become famous until the nineteenth century.

According to historical records, da Vinci began the painting in 1503, worked on it for four years, then moved to France, where he continued to work on it. Finally, after various stops and starts, he finished the work in 1519, the year he died.

Seeing that he spent sixteen years working on that one painting made me feel much better about my own personal overhaul. I wouldn't dare compare myself to da Vinci, of course, but if great works of art didn't follow a time schedule on their way to completion, I didn't see why the same couldn't be true of any kind of change or transformation in life, like love, weight loss, maintenance, spiritual enlightenment, and . . . getting my GED.

For all my enthusiasm about rushing back to school, however, I didn't end up enrolling in classes as quickly as I had planned. I didn't enroll, period. The days piled up with other things; weeks passed, and suddenly I didn't have enough time for such a big commitment. It would turn out to be one of those things I talked about for the next few months, and still talk about with every intention of following through before the end of 2010. I can get my diploma and AARP card at the same time.

Regardless, I'm prepared to work. I learned that lesson from my high school art teacher, Mr. Hamel. My transcript brought back that memory vividly. He had assigned the class to draw a still life in pencil. He brought in a collection of cereal boxes, paper towel cylinders, oatmeal canisters, tools, fruits, and vegetables for us to use in our composition. Instead, I chose something flat so I wouldn't have to worry about shading. I wanted to finish quickly but still do well enough to get an A.

Mr. Hamel made me pick something else. He said he knew what I was up to and wouldn't give me an easy A.

All these years later, I still catch myself occasionally looking for an easy A, except that I now know there aren't any shortcuts.

After sixteen months of dieting and maintenance, I had seen remarkable results. I had also learned that success couldn't be measured solely with a scale. In a lesson that many dieters learn too late or not at all, I discovered that the life I want isn't about reaching a single goal. More than losing 40 pounds, I really want a lightness of being, and now, more often than in the past, I feel it. But I have to keep working on myself to make it last.

My next challenge was to believe that I deserved to feel that good, and to continue to allow myself to get better.

Notes to Myself

❧

Despite an urge for cream sauce, I'm going to avoid it all day . . . and most likely survive.

Read the whole newspaper—not just the headlines!

"Wouldn't it be cool to be able to go back in time and actually walk alongside Jesus?" I asked Tom. I wonder if I had that thought because I was getting ready to shop for summer shoes and hoped I would find cute sandals. Any excuse . . .

Peace is a feeling in your heart that you can find even when you're in the middle of a hurricane.

Heard "Tiny Dancer" on the radio, and it reminded me of buying my first Elton John album thirty-five years ago. I hope I hold up as well as his music.

Part Two

Belief

Chapter Thirteen

What Matters

Most women tell similar stories of passing through their twenties, thirties, and forties, but when we hit that special age of fifty, all of a sudden, like my friend Amy, we can think of only one thing—a weekend blowout in Las Vegas. There, Tom and I joined a dozen or so couples for a weekend of partying, hanging out by the pool, a little gambling (we have a $100 limit), and lots of catching up with friends.

Months had passed since some of us had seen each other, while others of us talked all the time, but on the night the entire group got together in a private dining room to fete Amy, it was like everyone wanted to talk all at once about children, relationships, careers, politics. After a round of drinks and some more food, many of us gals ignored our men and got around to the stuff that was really on the minds of a group of women in their late forties and early fifties: our butts and boobs.

At that point, Tom didn't care who at the table knew how he felt about listening to a group of women talk about bras, eyebrows, and pre-menopausal changes. He blurted it right out: "Awkward!"

Not for me. I felt very lucky to be with women who know each other as intimately as we do in this group. Many of us had been friends since meeting in our kids' kindergarten class. We had sat together on the sidelines during soccer and Little League games, compared notes as we shepherded our kids through their driver's license tests, proms, and SATs. We had talked about our sex lives and laughed at the passage of time. We wondered, Where had it gone? Only a short time ago we were trading tips on toilet training. Now we were talking about hot flashes.

I told them about an old photo of Wolfie that I had found recently. The two of us were at the merry-go-round in Central Park. He was cuddled next to me, staring at me with complete adoration. I could see that he loved me unconditionally. That was the Wolfie I remembered. Not the current one who had a girlfriend, shaved, and got impatient when I warned him about abusing his credit card.

"I want *that* Wolfie back," I said.

Others told similar stories about their children. But we didn't really want those days back as much as we wanted to appreciate that time again. We wanted to compliment one another on jobs well done and reassure ourselves that we could get through the next stages of our lives without losing our minds, our health, or our friendships. We agreed that we were smarter now, wiser and better in nearly every way—and we looked damn good for our "age." These were good days, we agreed, and we hoped they would continue to be that way in the future.

I didn't want to be twenty-eight again, but neither did I feel like I was forty-eight. When my friends asked me how old I felt, I thought about asking if they meant my head, my knees, or my heart; I needed more specifics. Finally I said that I simply felt "older." And smarter. "But only sometimes." Which got a laugh.

Looking around the table, I saw that the common denominator among all of us was experience. We weren't old or older as much as we were experienced. Our different professions aside, we knew about giving birth, raising children, making doctor's appointments, nursing kids through various ailments, helping with homework. We knew how to feed a family every day, buy a car, and arrange financing for a home. We also knew about love, divorce, and survival. We knew about life.

We knew more than we gave ourselves credit for. All of a sudden, that seemed worth a round of toasts.

"When did age become more important than experience?" someone asked.

"Screw age," someone else said.

"Here's to experience!"

"And to wisdom."

"And to Advil!"

After dinner, we saw *Love*, the Cirque du Soleil show celebrating the music of the Beatles, and then we gambled. I played blackjack. I warned the girls I wasn't much of a gambler, but I realized that wasn't true about me—or any one of us making her way through life. With each decision, whether it is taking a job, starting a relationship, raising a child, or something as mundane as getting on an airplane, we all gamble to one degree or another that things will work out the way we want.

We do our best to stack the odds in our favor. We work out,

read books, eat healthy foods, see therapists, arrange for tutors, don't drink and drive, and fly on good airlines. The biggest bet of all is whether God is real and whether at some point we will have to answer for our thoughts and actions. Who knows?

Where better than a casino, and while holding a glass of white wine, to ponder whether you'll eventually meet your Maker and answer for your sins?

Back home, I focused on Wolfie's reapplication to private school. He had attended the school since kindergarten, but after he took off a year to go on tour, I was informed that he would have to reapply for his senior year. I had assumed it was a formality. The school knew us, and who would separate a kid from his friends for his last year in high school without good cause? But I didn't know for sure.

Then there was the X factor—me. For months, I had ignored a To-Do note on my computer. I clicked it away every time it popped up on the screen, reminding me to fill out the application, which was just a couple of short essay questions. I frequently *thought* about filling it out. Several times I got as far as clicking the URL, opening up the file, and reading the questions. But then I would go back to ignoring it.

Finally I figured out the reason for my block, one that I'm sure has driven many mothers to the brink of craziness: I had made it more about me than Wolfie.

I had to come clean with myself. My problem was a bout of raging insecurity. I was, like, Welcome back, old friend. Who let you in? In all seriousness, where had the confident forty-eight-year-old who was toasting experience in Vegas gone? All of a sudden I had turned into Sally Field before she won the Oscar for

Norma Rae. I was in the kitchen, hoping to get an envelope that would allow me to say, "You like me! You really like me!" After seventeen years of mothering Wolfie, I wanted that re-admittance letter as validation that I had done a good job as his mom.

I still wasn't sure that I had made the right decision by taking him out of school for eleventh grade so he could go on tour. I felt that I should turn the application into a confession. Forget the questions on the form. I would simply write the truth:

> *Dear Admissions Office:*
>
> *Before I screw up my son's education the same way I did my own, please accept him back in school for twelfth grade. I want him to get his diploma, something I never managed to accomplish, and it bugs me to this day. Also, in addition to re-admitting him, I'd like you to reassure me that I didn't make a mistake last year by taking him out of school and that I'm not a bad mother.*
>
> *Sincerely,*
> *Valerie Bertinelli, Wolfie's mom*

When I finally sat down at my desk, I stared at the blank screen, searching for a way to start. I had no idea how to write about my child. One problem was what to say. Another was where to start. The things that came immediately to mind were the things that made me want to wring his neck, and the stories I thought were most endearing and worth sharing had happened between the ages of four and eight. Neither would've been appropriate. The school knew him well. In fact, he had probably spent more time there since kindergarten than he had at home.

Tom came in and saw me staring at the photos I have of Wolfie taped to my desk, including an adorable snapshot of him in his yellow-and-blue soccer uniform. My eyes drifted over the table to the left of my desk where I had a framed black-and-white photo of me in a blousy shirt and black underwear when I was eight-and-a-half months pregnant. It might be the sexiest picture I've ever taken.

"Just start," said Tom, who stood behind me and rubbed my shoulders for a few moments. Then he left and inspiration hit. "Of course," I said.

On the application, I explained why Wolfie had left the school. I also described his strengths and challenges as a student. With the basics then out of the way, I opened up my heart and addressed the thing that had frightened me in the first place: how this related to me. It was undeniable. If someone asked me how I most identified myself, it would be as not as an actress or spokesperson but as Wolfie's mom. Most people at that school knew me that way, too. I could not fathom that part of my life ending yet.

I explained how being part of that school provided both of us with a sense of community and family. While I emphasized the part the school played in Wolfie's life, I realized it was equally important in mine. In light of my personal evolution and the more recent talks I'd had with my girlfriends at Amy's birthday party in Las Vegas, I saw how vital it was to feel part of a community and connected to people. Our lives were intertwined. They helped give me my identity as a mother. As a person, they kept me afloat on bad days and made the good days even better.

Clichéd or not, it was true. How could I have ever not known what to write? How could they not let him back in?

Years earlier, my dad had been going through old boxes of family heirlooms that he and my mom had carted around from house to house. After storing some of that stuff for fifty years, he was finally parceling it out to us kids. Among the things I ended up with that day was my grandmother's rosary. It's one of my most treasured possessions, something I always have in my purse. In fact, it's always the first thing I transfer when I change purses. I keep it in its original pouch with a red crocheted cross she made long ago, and whenever I look inside I feel a special, immediate connection to my grandmother.

I didn't feel quite the same thing when I thought about Wolfie's school, but it was similar in that the connections run deep and are very personal and laden with memories. Having made that happy association for myself, I could have clocked Wolfie one day when he asked if he really had to go back for twelfth grade.

Up till then, he had been inquiring if we'd heard any news about his re-admission. Seeing my exasperated face, he said, "Don't get mad. I was just wondering if it mattered."

Don't get mad?

Did it matter?

Wolfie had rendered me temporarily mute, which was rare. As I worked my way through feelings of shock, anger, and downright stupefaction, I considered sanely explaining the importance of an education. I also thought I might remind him of the insecurity I had carried around from not having a high school diploma, not to mention how hard a time I was currently having getting back on track to get my GED. I thought about many things I could have said to him, and then I thought I could have Tom speak to him, too.

But I didn't want to explain some of these things for the one hundredth time. I wouldn't let myself. So I said, "Why does it matter? Because it does."

"But why?" he asked.

"Because I said so."

"But why?"

Suddenly I understood. Realizing he was playing a game with me, I called his bluff.

"Do you really want to know?" I asked.

"No," he said. "I believe you."

Not long after that, I heard from Wolfie's school. He was readmitted. I thanked God. Tom thought I had worried more than was necessary, and I'm sure he was right, but I couldn't help it. We celebrated by going out to a nice dinner. Before we went out, I changed purses, and the first thing I transferred was my grandmother's rosary.

Notes to Myself

How come the girl passing out the Cinnabon samples at the mall is thin?

Remind yourself to go to the farmers' market this Sunday. There's nothing like eating fresh, locally grown, and healthy food. It's a treat for the body.

I've been thinking about food more than I should through some stressful times, and I have to remind myself that food is food. Don't give it any more power than it has, and don't give it any power that I have myself.

Your attitude decides whether you are happy or not. You can change your attitude.—Paramahansa Yogananda

Believe in the good stuff.

Chapter Fourteen

Back to Work

"So, have you thought more about getting into a bikini?" asked Jenny Craig executive Scott Parker.

I pushed back from the table and laughed. I knew the question would come sooner or later. The Jenny Craig marketing execs with whom I worked had dropped hints for months. But I didn't expect it would be put forth as bluntly as it was at that moment. It was early September, and my managers, Jack and Marc, and I were meeting with the company's executives about extending my contract. They wanted two years and a guarantee from me that I would pose in a bikini.

I liked the idea of two years. It promised security, as well as monthly weigh-ins. But I didn't want to guarantee anything in my life, especially that I'd step in front of a camera in a skimpy, two-piece bathing suit.

"I'm thinking about it," I said. "But I don't want to commit."

Truth be told, I had already made up my mind. I knew that I was going to eventually get into a bikini. I didn't know when. I didn't like the idea of a timetable that I didn't set. But I knew that I was going to do it.

It was my secret. I had decided six months earlier when I was in Hawaii with Tom, shooting my surfing commercial. After we finished, Tom and I stayed an extra day to shoot a segment for the *Rachael Ray* show. They had flown out a vivacious young police officer who had lost a significant amount of weight and wanted to wear a bikini for the first time. According to the plan, I was supposed to provide her with the you-go-girl type of encouragement she needed to get into a skimpy two-piece and show off her new body. But she didn't need any prodding from me. She put on her bikini, slipped off her robe, and paraded in front of everyone without any inhibition. She had worked her ass off to lose weight and was more than ready to let the world see her remarkable before-and-after transformation. I just stood back and watched. She was so ballsy and fun. Her face said everything: "I am here. I am hot. And I like myself."

Instead of following the script line of my inspiring her, she inspired me. Before we finished the segment, I confided that I secretly wanted to do what she had done. I wanted to get my butt in a bikini, too. But—

She didn't give me time to finish.

"You can do it," she said.

Until then, I honestly didn't know if I could. But seeing her sashay confidently and proudly in her tiny bathing suit planted a seed. One thing about me, I can't resist a challenge, especially one I pose for myself.

However, I had another question. Did I *want* to get in a bikini?

I didn't know how much work it would take, but I had spent nearly a year losing 40 pounds and I knew that even that wasn't enough to be in bikini shape for me. I also knew that no matter what was required, I was going to have to do more than get into the best shape of my life. The challenges would also be mental and emotional, as well as physical.

I stood on the beach by myself fast-forwarding through my thoughts and didn't notice Tom come up alongside me just as I muttered, "You know what? I'm going to do it."

He bumped his shoulder into mine and asked, "Huh?"

I put my hand over my mouth and gasped, "Oh, shit, why did I say that?"

"What are you talking about?"

"Nothing," I said.

But obviously that wasn't true. I knew. I just wasn't ready to tell anyone, even Tom.

Now, six months later, I wasn't any more ready to commit publicly. I definitely wasn't ready to sign on the dotted line. I was still maneuvering around the idea in my mind—what it would mean, what it would take, and how long I would need.

I take a long time between making a decision and heeding the call to action. I have never been one to rush into anything. As I have stated numerous times, it took me seventeen years to figure out how unhappy I was in my marriage and what my options were, and then I needed another three years before I did anything about it. A bikini would be no different. I hadn't been in one since I was twenty years old. Now, at forty-eight, even though deep down I knew it would happen, I didn't see any reason to rush.

Like any great procrastinator, I was able to rationalize whatever time it was going to take. Hey, God could have flooded the world in a few hours if He had wanted. After all, He was God. But he took care of business over forty days and forty nights. That was enough of an example for me. I would take whatever time I needed.

As I have learned, time has a way of allowing things to work out the way they are supposed to, although not necessarily or always the way you want. For example, a few weeks after my meeting with the Jenny Craig folks, I began work on a pilot for TBS, a sitcom known at the network as the *Untitled Dave Caplan Project*. Writer and executive producer Dave Caplan, a veteran of the *Drew Carey* and *George Lopez* shows, was a curly-haired *mensch* whose script was a warm, hilarious love letter to the relationship he'd had with his mother when he was seventeen.

I had wanted to get back into comedy and I stepped into the role as if it was a favorite pair of shoes. The mother-son dynamic at the show's core was sweet, warm, and close to my heart. During the casting process, I came home one night after a long day of readings with other actors. I fell into a chair and took a deep breath, collecting myself finally after a long day. I hadn't been as tired or felt as good in ages. Tom asked how my day had been.

"You know what?" I said. "My day was blessed."

"Really?" he asked, momentarily surprised by my answer, which he might have expected to be a simple "great" or "fine" or "good except for the traffic."

"That's great," he said.

"It is great," I said. "I feel blessed."

For the next few weeks, I immersed myself in the sweat and toil of helping to make a TV show. I worked with Dave to flesh out the character and find the laughs. I read with the other actors as casting decisions were finalized, and then I read with the cast, a talented group that included Nadia Dajani, Kevin Schmidt, and stand-up comic Anjelah Johnson, who blew me away from the moment I saw her audition tape and then again when I read with her.

Everyone on the set except for me seemed to have watched and re-watched her routine bit about a nail salon, that had millions of hits on YouTube. I went home, watched it, and became an instant devotee of that as well as her *MadTV* character Bon Qui-Qui, a fast-food counter girl with major attitude. On top of being gorgeous, Anjelah had perfect timing. I had to try my hardest not to crack up when we worked together. She also hit it off with Tom, who fell in love when he tasted her homemade salsa and chips.

Three years earlier, I had auditioned for another TBS series, *The Bill Engvall Show*, and been told thanks, but no thanks. When I didn't get the job, I thought my career had finally sputtered to an end, and with it, my income, which I sorely needed since I had chosen not to take any alimony or child support from Ed in the divorce. My ass was really tossed on the ground—and even though it didn't feel like it at the time, it was the best thing that had happened to me.

In hindsight, had I gotten the job, just as had I asked for money from Ed, I never would have taken the call from Jenny Craig, lost weight, regained my self-confidence, self-esteem, and sense of hope, nor would I have been available for this exciting opportunity on *The Untitled Dave Caplan Show*.

One day on the set, I flashed on all that. I saw where I easily could have still been: trying to lose fifteen or twenty pounds, yo-yoing up and down physically and emotionally, as I had done for years. I would have been employed and had a steady income, but been stuck in a place where I knew my life was not working as I would have liked. I never would have faced what was broken in me.

Now I was overwhelmed by all the good stuff happening to

me, almost to the point that I could barely handle it. Where was the booby trap? Why didn't I believe I deserved it? Why did I still occasionally go to the dark place where I worried that things were too good and bound to end in catastrophe?

I buoyed myself by talking to God. I thanked Him for the goodness in my life, the big and the little stuff. I also thanked Him for giving me one more day without the meteor hitting. I didn't yet see that I was equally if not more responsible for these blessings.

Wolfie was asking his own why's, too. In the days before he began his senior year of high school, he again wanted to know why he needed to go back to school. We had long talks about the importance of an education. I drew on my own experience, a story he had heard many times before, but he listened to it again and again, seeming to accept my position that his diploma, while seemingly unimportant now, would be meaningful to him in the future.

He didn't argue past the first day, but returned to school and fell back in step with his friends and his classes. I claimed that as a win. Who knew, maybe he would continue on to college and study music.

Between my work, Wolfie's school, Tom's business, and his shuttling back and forth to Arizona, life got even more hectic for all of us, and especially me as the household's chief cook, bottle washer, and worrywart. I sensed how easy it would be to deal with the ebb and flow of anxiety by reverting to old bad habits. It was a reminder that I would always have good and bad days, days when I was stronger, as well as days when fatigue and worry could weaken my resistance to the gut-warming lure of a cheeseburger.

Awareness was the first line of defense against any slips. I knew myself better than I had a year earlier, and I liked myself more, too.

I wanted to stay on track. In addition, I helped my cause by stocking my dressing room with Jenny Craig food, including a basket of snacks so that I would always have something when the rest of the cast and crew hit the snack table during breaks. I worked out diligently and kept to my daily schedule even when I was tired.

As a result, I was able to focus on the right things as we made the pilot. Rehearsal and shooting stretched over eight days, with the last one in front of a live audience, making it the most amazing of all our workdays. The audience bought in to the characters, and they laughed hard throughout the taping. Not since *One Day at a Time* had I felt as comfortable in front of the camera. More importantly I felt that I was exactly where I should be, doing the thing I loved most, which was making people laugh.

I got home and thanked God for giving me such a gift, as well as so many others, including my family, my health, and a sense that almost anything was possible. However, on the chance my luck was about to run out, I asked Him to let me know if I should brace for an onslaught of frogs or locusts. I didn't want to wake up one day and say to myself, "I told you so," because I had given away all my size 12s.

God didn't work that way, Tom explained, laughing at me. I knew he was right. My concern that none of this good stuff that was happening to me would last was really a matter of needing to believe in myself. I just had to get used to the new me.

After finishing the pilot, I suffered the natural let-down of no longer going to work and seeing people whose company I had grown to enjoy. Actors know that can be jarring and painful. But it was out of my control. The pilot had to be edited, go through post-production, and then move to the network for testing and review.

None of us knew how long it would take TBS execs to provide feedback and decide whether they were going to order more episodes.

As it turned out, I didn't have to wait long before going back in front of the camera. The man in charge of casting Dave Caplan's pilot also worked on *Boston Legal*, one of my favorite TV shows. During the taping, I had asked him to please, please, please tell *Boston*'s brilliant creator-producer David E. Kelly that I loved the show, had wanted to be on it for years, and would play anything if he would write me onto an episode before it went off the air, which the series was about to do.

Soon after I got a call that David had written a part for me. Again, I couldn't believe my luck. How fun was it going to be?! I pinched myself. I was flummoxed, and yet again, I talked to God. I wanted to know what parallel universe I was in that I was getting such amazing grace in my life.

Tom advised me to quit worrying when my luck might run out, because the good stuff that was freaking me out was based on hard work and good, healthy decisions. He suggested that I set new goals, continue challenging myself, and realize the bread I was casting on the water might be as sweet as French toast.

His words were particularly meaningful when my managers, Jack and Marc, called and said they needed to conclude contract talks with Jenny Craig. They had only one more point to address. They said I had to decide whether or not I would agree to an ad campaign featuring me getting into a bikini.

As close as I was to both of them, they still had no idea that I had made my decision months earlier. What I realized, though, was that it was finally time for me to come out of hiding— figuratively and literally. I told them that I would try. But I didn't want to promise. I gave them my reasons for not making a full commitment and then requested we aim for the next spring. I would need the time and probably wouldn't begin training in earnest until after the holidays.

I was only trying to be realistic. Besides, given that we were talking about a bikini, some wiggle room seemed appropriate.

Notes to Myself

✧

Go somewhere new this weekend. Find a cool street to walk around or explore a new area. Just not a new ice cream shop.

Read more books! Learning is food for thought—and zero calories.

20,000 steps—and try to get 5,000 more.

Maintenance is just a continuation of what I did yesterday, but a little bit more and a little bit different . . .

Conscience is God's presence in man.—Emanual Swedenborg

Chapter Fifteen

Questions

As soon as I heard that the themes of Maria Shriver's California Women's Conference were empowerment, transformation, and motivation, I accepted the invitation to participate. But once I arrived at the one-day event at the Long Beach convention center, I was intimidated. For starters, there was the size of the crowd. The fourteen thousand seats had sold out in three hours, and then Maria, in her opening address, estimated that more than a million women could also log on via streaming video. I wasn't used to being in front of that many people.

Then there were the other participants, the real stars, including Maria's husband, California Governor Arnold Schwarzenegger, Secretary of State Condoleezza Rice, Jennifer Lopez, Warren Buffett, Sister Joan Chittister, and Bono, who could move tens of thousands of people with a single wave of his finger. I had been invited to interview my friend Rachael Ray, but as we took the stage, part of me was wondering why the hell was I sharing a stage with that heady group?

I wanted to be out in the audience. I was a sponge when it came to absorbing life lessons from those who had put themselves on the line and returned with genuine wisdom. It was as though they had opened windows that let me see a little more clearly and farther down the road. I realized I was hungry and curious, and unlike the way I basically ignored such urges when I was at my worst, I listened to that voice telling me to learn and grow, and I went with it.

I let that shape my point of view as I settled in opposite Rachael and began firing questions at her. I felt I knew her well enough from appearing on her show so often. But I had no idea how she had actually become Rachael Ray the star and business-woman. So as thousands watched, I decided to satisfy my curiosity, and I found out that Rachael's first show, *30-Minute Meals*, had begun as a cooking class that she taught in a grocery story in Albany, New York.

"I was trying to get people to buy more groceries," she said.

In those days, Rachael was a food buyer. But when she noticed that customers weren't buying the great foods and ingredients she brought into the store, she asked them why and found out they simply didn't know how to cook with them. With the kind of prac-ticality that would become her trademark, she began cooking dem-onstrations in the store. The rest was hard work from there to her own show.

"It didn't just happen," she said. "I loved the work, and I think if you love what you do the magic part happens organically. You tend to get noticed whether you're a dish machine operator—my first job—a waitress, a manager, or something else. If you love what you do, you'll want to do it all day long and you'll smile through the day."

If I hadn't been onstage and dressed in a conservative business suit, fulfilling a decidedly professional role, I might have jumped up and shrieked, "Exactly!" I also might have elaborated my feelings that such lessons applied to more than work. The same was true about the rest of one's life. As I had discovered and continued to learn, if you make a conscious effort to live your life in a way that makes you love it, despite the inevitable bad days, the magic will happen.

Maria had set an inspirational tone earlier in the day, opening the conference by stating that it was okay to not have it all figured out. By "it all," we knew she meant life, our roles as wives, mothers, businesswomen, children of aging parents, concerned citizens, and, generally, as women. She pointed to herself and said she didn't have all the answers. None of us did, which was a comforting realization, as was the awareness that came when you looked around the hall and at the people on the stage and saw that everyone had gathered to share unique areas of expertise and life experiences with the intention of helping each other figure things out.

I didn't expect to get the complete picture, but every little bit of knowledge and insight helped, just as losing a pound or two a week on a diet helps. Over a year or two or ten, I realized, it adds up. It's called wisdom.

Morning session host Deborah Norville followed Maria and asked everyone to turn off her cell phone and BlackBerry and begin the day with a moment of quiet.

"Only still can be still," she said, quoting a Chinese proverb.

I loved the concept of starting the day with a moment of introspective silence. For most people, a typical day begins with the sound of an alarm, a dance to the toilet, forty-five minutes of music blasting during exercise, the rush to shower, twenty minutes of news on TV, e-mail, then traffic, ringing phones, meetings, and so on; the noise builds steadily throughout the day and doesn't stop. Then at night we employ various methods of trying to turn the volume back down.

I wondered what it would be like if more of us began the day by listening to the music of silence or the sound of the human heart. What would it be like if I began my day with a moment of silence?

I knew the answer.

I would hear me—my inner voice and the sound of my heart.

Without getting too Gandhi, as Wolfie often accuses me of doing, let me say I am awestruck every time I hear my heart beat. It reminds me to avoid anything that might mess it up. The regularity of that thump-thump keeping me alive, as it does every human being, is also the drumbeat that keeps me on course in every aspect of my life, not just my diet and maintenance. My challenge is to listen to it.

To me, the most awe-inspiring part about hearing my heartbeat is the knowledge that it sounds the same in every other woman. It's the song that connects all of us no matter what race, religion, and nationality we are. The joy I feel in my heart when my son does something good is no different from the joy a mother on the other side of the world feels when her child does something that makes her proud. It's the same with feelings of pain, grief, and love.

And so I made a pledge to try to start my day with a moment of quiet in the hope of hearing the voice and music in me more clearly.

• • •

Jennifer Lopez also took the stage, and she could have been talking directly to me when she asked, "Are we truly present?"

"I was really honored to come here and speak to you because I get to stand here not as an entertainer, but as a girl who grew up in the Bronx with two sisters and a strong and loving mom. I realized early in my own journey that I had to be my own champion. Nobody told me to do what I did—most told me not to do it. But I was lucky enough to have a strong feeling inside that I should listen to my gut and it would guide me. When I didn't listen is when I had my biggest mishaps."

"Certain relationships make you doubt who you are and what you're capable of and what you deserve," she continued. "It took me some time to get it right in that arena. That's why I'm telling you. You have to listen to that voice. In one of my lowest moments, when I didn't have a grasp of who I was or where I was going, I prayed for guidance, for strength, a message, something. I picked up my Bible and the passage said, 'Be happy for your trials and tribulations because you test your faith.' "

Following Jennifer, Disney-ABC Television President Anne Sweeney delivered another inspiring call to action, saying that each person had "the power to be an architect of change.

"By being who we truly are, we can make a difference," she said. "We can all be leaders in our own lives and communities. You'll hear a lot of variations on that theme today. For me, it's a great reminder that we actually control our own destiny, that we choose the life we lead."

I didn't just agree, I was proof. MSNBC anchor Chris Matthews noted that women owned half of all small businesses and that that number was growing faster than in any other sector.

Women make 80 percent of all buying decisions and influence an even higher percentage. Later, CNN journalist Christiane Amanpour provided a more global view, praising women entrepreneurs for making strides in Africa where men succeed only in killing each other off.

Backstage, I posed with Maria for pictures. I hadn't seen her in a very long time—not since she had interviewed me in the early 1980s. I complimented her for bringing all these women together and providing a place where all of us gals could say to each other, "We can do this!"

It was the first time I had been a part of an event like that, and I hoped not the last. As I told Maria, I would be returning home as changed, inspired, and motivated as anyone who had bought a ticket, and I meant it.

After the photos, I signed books in another area of the convention hall, a cavernous room set up with booths and filled with women waiting in line to meet other authors. I enjoyed personalizing books and listening to stories and memories they wanted to share. I have heard people complain about such tasks. I'm not trying to sound like a goody-goody, but I like making these connections and finding out how similarly most of us live. I get strength and encouragement—and quite a few laughs.

I was having a fun time, and then it got even better when I glanced at a neighboring table and recognized *The Biggest Loser* trainer Jillian Michaels, who was also signing books. She had more people waiting in line for her than anyone else. I understood. I wanted to get in her line, too. I am a huge fan of hers.

At that point, Tom and my managers and a couple of the executives at Jenny Craig were the only people aware that I was thinking about getting into a bikini. Suddenly, though, I wanted to tell Jillian about it. More specifically, I wanted to ask if she could help get me into shape—the kind of shape where I would be comfortable exposing that much of my body to myself, never mind the public.

I kept my eye on Jillian as I continued signing books. I didn't want her getting away before I spoke to her.

"Damn, that woman is in amazing shape," I said to Tom as I marveled at Jillian's body.

As much as I wanted to talk to her, I was too shy to approach her. I knew what it was like to work at one of these events and then need to leave so you could get back to your life. Tom thought I was being way too sissified—that was the word he used. In fact, when I turned around to say hello to Rita Wilson, Tom sneaked off and introduced himself to Jillian. He explained the situation.

She came straight over to me, explained that she knew what was going on, and said, "You look good enough to put on a bikini now."

"No way," I said, embarrassed.

"Well, no worries. I'll get your ass in a bikini."

I couldn't believe the B-word was now being spoken out loud. B-I-K-I-N-I. In the context of the conference, amid all these women wanting to inspire or be inspired, it seemed appropriate. Seeing Jillian nearby was like a cherry on top of the sundae, or like a sign from God. My inner voice—the one Jennifer Lopez had urged us to listen to—was going nuts. On the one hand, it said, "Pray she really will help you." On the other, it added, "But no matter what, make sure there's a wrap around your ass."

A couple of weeks later, Jillian and I met for lunch. I was too inhibited to order anything on my own lest she snap, "You're ordering that? That stuff will kill you." If she'd done that, I would have died. To be safe, I decided to order the same thing she did—whatever it was. She could not have been nicer, though, and I instantly felt like I had made a new friend.

Sadly for me, she had no time to train me or anyone else. Her work on *The Biggest Loser* and related projects kept her too busy for any private clients. But in a stroke of both genius and generosity, she whipped out her cell phone and called her friend Christopher. She said that she had a project for him. They chatted, she mentioned my name, she said the B-word, and then she hung up and looked at me.

"Everything's set."

What was set? Who was this Christopher?

It turned out Christopher was Jillian's friend and trainer. Hearing that she sometimes had help in the gym surprised me.

"Someone trains you?"

She laughed. "Yes."

Of course she did. Why wouldn't she?

It dawned on me that life is a series of questions and answers—but mostly questions. It was only by asking questions that you got to the answers. When I thought back to my darkest days, I realized that I began to climb out of them when I asked myself the question that was then the biggest question of my life: did I plan to spend the rest of my days miserable, lying in bed at night and over-eating?

More questions followed: Did I feel healthy? If not, why? What were the best decisions I'd made? What were the worst? What were the ramifications of those bad decisions? What had worked in my life? What hadn't? What was currently working? What wasn't? And what was I going to do about it? What *could* I do?

Later, as I thought about the interview I had done with Rachael, I realized that I liked asking questions more than I did responding to them. But that made me also realize that even though I had trouble coming up with answers that I believed in—I had few answers, in fact—that was okay.

As Maria Shriver had said earlier, it was okay not to know all the answers or to have everything figured out. We are expected to know so much, and yet in reality can't possibly know it all. I absolutely loved giving myself permission to stop trying to figure it all out.

Once I did that, I eliminated about twelve thousand things from the list of things I normally worried about, which meant I got rid of about twelve thousand things that usually made me want to eat. It was like a giant exhale.

I felt the weight melt off my shoulders. I hoped it would melt off my thighs, too. I hoped I would hear from Christopher.

Notes to Myself

❧

I don't know why, but I had to remind Wolfie to brush his teeth today. Tom added, "Brush only the ones you want to keep." Ha!

I alone am responsible for my actions. Therefore I have to remember to make them actions that are beneficial to me— and the rest of the world.

Be kind, for everyone you meet is fighting the hard battle.
—Phyllo of Alexandria

Chapter Sixteen

Heart of the Matter

I felt a sudden, sickening surge of dread and anxiety when I got a call that my mom was seriously ill. I was in New York, taping another appearance on the *Rachael Ray* show, when my brother Patrick tracked me down and gave me the news, which was developing so quickly that I felt like a CNN reporter in the field.

My parents had gone on a cruise to the Caribbean and had been at sea for a couple of days when my mom got sick. Her condition worsened quickly; the shipboard doctor determined it was her long-simmering heart-valve condition. From what my brother told me, she was fairly calm as the ordeal developed. I wasn't surprised, as that is so in my mom's character.

The ship's crew was also prepared for such emergencies and kept her stable and comfortable until they got to a nearby island in the Florida Keys where she was taken off the ship and driven by ambulance to a small hospital. There, she was put in a bed in the emergency room next to a guy who'd been gravely injured in a motorcycle accident. As she watched doctors work on him, she realized her own situation was also serious.

It was like a nightmare. After examining her, doctors pinpointed the problem as her bad heart valve and said she needed surgery. They weren't equipped to perform such a major operation. They suggested she transfer to one of the larger cities in Florida. My father wanted her own doctors to do the operation in Arizona, which created another problem: how to get her home? None of the airlines would fly someone in her condition. As I said, it was a nightmare.

In the meantime, I was racing through my life in a way that challenged the calendar function on my computer. I kept cramming more and more onto my schedule. Wolfie was also in rehearsals for his school play *Death Trap*; Tony had gotten a job; and Tom was juggling work, me, and trips to Scottsdale to see his kids.

Then, wham-o: my brother called with the news about my mom, and suddenly time stopped. When it started again, nothing else mattered except my mom. I was constantly on the phone with my dad or my brothers, asking questions that didn't have easy answers. What did the airlines say? Have you talked to her doctor? What do they think? How's she doing?

Through this rough time of not knowing anything, we constantly sought updates and offered emotional support to my dad, as well as any other kind of support he needed. He was downright heroic. He kept my mom calm, monitored the island doctors, kept my mom's doctor back home informed, and worked the phones, trying to find a way to get her back to Arizona.

I was unsure of what else to do with them more than three thousand miles away. I coped by cleaning the house and then

straightening up what I had just cleaned. I pushed worst-case scenarios out of my head and spent time thinking about the way my
mom had run the house when I was little, making full breakfasts
for five people in the morning, having lunches set out, and then
making delicious three-course dinners at night. The woman had
made chicken four thousand different ways. She had also kept the
house immaculate. Her skill and efficiency now seemed implau-
sible to me.

But so did this whole situation. We Bertinellis were slow-
moving and fairly conservative. We didn't have emergencies. As a
result, I felt ill-equipped, frustrated for not being able to do more,
and impatient. I wanted to do something, but there wasn't anything that could be done.

I said a lot of prayers. I even prayed that I wasn't overloading
God with too many prayers. I was like that girlfriend who can't
stop calling: "Hey, it's me again."

Finally, my brother called with good news. He said that my
dad had worked out a way to air-vac my mom to Arizona, where
her open-heart surgery was already scheduled. We weren't out of
the woods yet by any means. But all of a sudden I felt hopeful.

My brothers Pat and David picked me up at Phoenix's Sky Harbor
airport and took me straight to the hospital. We were able to visit
with my mom before her operation. She was weak but ready and
confident. I wish I could have said the same about me. As we sat
with her, my brothers and I tried not to show how scared we were.
My dad, despite a brave face, was also frightened.

I understood. He and my mom had been together fifty-
plus years. I tried to imagine all the thoughts going through his
head.

Funny enough, it was my mom who reassured us that she would come through the operation. She had faith in her doctors, who were very positive. She also reminded us that she had spent the past few years losing nearly 50 pounds and exercising herself into better shape to prepare for this exact procedure, which for years she had known would be inevitable. She gave us the thumbs up.

In that touching little moment, I was reminded of how important it was to learn to appreciate your life before you get to the point where my mom was, lying in a hospital bed and putting your fate in the hands of doctors. My mom was way ahead of me.

As we gathered in the waiting room, I knew that she was going to make it. I wasn't filled with a dreadful sense of imminent bad news. I trusted that instinct. Nevertheless, I was scared and ready to cry at any moment. I was most unsettled from seeing my dad so worried and vulnerable. He was a man who had always been in charge, and now he wasn't.

Thank goodness the signs on the wall prohibited food and beverages in the area. I was sure the hospital officials who had put them there knew that most people coped with stressful situations, and especially surgeries, by eating, and if left to themselves, the waiting room would likely resemble a herd of cows grazing in a field of Cheetos and cookies.

I drew support and comfort from being with my dad, my two brothers, and my sister-in-law Stacy. No one goes through life alone, and this was proof of how much we needed one another, especially family. In some ways, it was, if not a bonding experience, an opportunity to re-bond. We told stories from our childhoods, remembered good times, and shared laughs that we might not have otherwise had.

In a way, it was like an answered prayer. I had prayed for

strength and God had delivered a way for all of us to get through this ordeal without breaking down into a million pieces. He'd brought our family together, and the five of us made each other stronger.

After about four hours, my mom's surgeon walked into the waiting room still wearing his surgical scrubs. He told my dad that Mom had made it through the surgery without a single glitch and was still asleep in ICU. All of us huddled around so we could hear. Then we hugged my dad and each other.

Early the next day, I went for a power walk before going back to the hospital to see my mom. She was on major pain medication, but doing much better than I'd expected, given that it had been less than twenty-four hours since surgeons pulled her chest open, took out her heart, attached new valves, and then put everything back together. Talk about miracles. I needed weeks just to rearrange my pantry.

I also marveled at my mom's attitude as much as I did at modern medicine. She had never doubted that she would come through, and her belief had provided the rest of us with faith and hope, the two keys to everything. She had lost weight to give herself the best chance of surviving the major operation she knew she had to have—and when it was time, she approached it as if she were going to sail through because she still had a lot of living she wanted to do.

Still, it was jarring to see her hooked up to monitors in the ICU and waiting to be moved to her own room, so after leaving the hospital I finally opened my tear ducts and let myself cry.

Like it or not, all of us are going to reach the end someday. It's non-negotiable. But we do have a choice about *how* we live. We can either wait for the end in a gloomy funk, carping and complaining, blaming and bitching; or we can approach each day as if it's an opportunity to feel good and do better, and to be more patient, forgiving, and helpful.

Less than a week later, my mom was moved into a private room. I stuck around a few more days, then flew home and caught up on everything that I had put on hold. Tom reminded me that I was in time to see all four of Wolfie's performances in the school play. He saw me grimace and gave me a bear hug.

"It's going to be great," he said.

"But how come his father only has to go to one performance and I have to go to all four?"

"Because you're his mom."

He was right. My mom had driven me to every rehearsal and taping of *One Day at a Time* for almost six years—until I turned eighteen and didn't need a guardian on the set anymore. I went to Wolfie's shows and participated enthusastically in the standing ovation all of the parents and relatives and friends gave after each performance. As Tom can attest, even though I might have complained once or twice and mentioned that I had already seen the original on Broadway, the truth is, I'm a softie—and I enjoyed every minute of it.

Notes to Myself

❧

Have to start working out in preparation for Thanksgiving. What if it was called "Giving Thanks"?

I have to remind myself that exercise is not the enemy even if it makes me smell bad. In fact, B.O. is the smell of progress.

I can already feel the holiday stress. Remember it takes two to make an argument. So bite your tongue and work on patience and compromise. It's easier than waiting for everyone else to realize they were wrong and need to apologize—ha!

Quick thought: There is plenty of food. But time is limited. Why waste it feeling bad?

Chapter Seventeen

Yes, We Can

Normally I turn my attention to Thanksgiving about a week or ten days before Turkey Day actually arrives. That's usually enough time to confirm which family members are able to show up, organize who will cook what, and start working out a little harder in preparation for the annual feast. But this year I began thinking about the holiday as soon as I flipped my calendar to November.

As far as I was concerned, I had more to be thankful for this year, starting with my mother's recovery, which was going as planned. Everybody else was great. My life was moving forward, my weight was still down, and I was about to tackle a new goal that would get me in even better shape. Then there was Obama, who looked as if he was about to become America's next president. Like so many millions of Americans, I was swept up in the excitement and hope of change.

With all the time I was spending in Arizona, though, I was

careful not to say Barack Obama's name out loud around my father. My dad had gone through a hard enough time with my mother's surgery. I didn't know if he could handle a Democrat in the White House.

I wanted to assure him it would be okay. I really wanted to say, "Don't worry. He couldn't do any worse than Bush and Cheney." But the truth of the matter was, my dad and I avoided the subject as much as possible, which was not an easy task since we spent most of the time sitting with my mother, watching TV. And they liked to watch the news. They knew everything that was going on, from the major headlines to the minor stories and the scuffles that served as filler.

The trouble was, they preferred Fox News. Despite my dad's long marriage and devotion to my mom, I sometimes felt that he had a stronger relationship with Bill O'Reilly. On the other hand, I preferred reading *The Week*. More than once, I heard my mom say, "Andy, don't watch Fox in front of Valerie. She'll put a hex on us."

The upcoming election was all any of us talked about, but we didn't do it too much when we were together. With other topics scarce, I told my parents that I was thinking about getting into a bikini in the spring for a new Jenny Craig ad campaign. I even managed to make it seem politically inspired.

"Really?" my dad said.

"Yup . . ."

"How do you feel about that?"

"It's a time for hope," I said.

My mom laughed.

"Good for you," she said.

Actually I had decided that I wouldn't start working earnestly to get into bikini shape until after the election, Thanksgiving dinner (and leftovers), and Christmas. Based on my previous conversation with Jillian Michaels, I suspected that I would have to train like an athlete to get my body into a place where I felt comfortable seeing myself in a bikini, the prerequisite before I stepped in front of a camera; and I didn't think I could buckle down with the temptation of holiday goodies.

I knew I could do it, though. I loved a good challenge, setting goals, and reaching them, as well as the idea of transformation and growth—what Obama referred to as change. It may seem silly, but I felt a little like I was plugged into a new trend that was sweeping America partly by choice and mostly by necessity. It was the idea of reinvention.

Obama spoke about it on a national scale, but also related it to individuals. In a way, I was one of those people, not all that different from the workers on Wall Street or at Ford or GM, where my father had worked most of his life. They were experiencing hard times. Everything they knew and counted on for decades had changed, broken, or closed altogether. Lives that had been stable were full of uncertainty. It was scary.

I had gone through a similar situation a few years earlier when my career seemed to have dried up, my income was nonexistent, I had to dip into my savings way more than I was comfortable doing, and I was fat and unhappy with myself. I didn't know what to do. But I knew enough to recognize that my life wasn't working and that somehow, someway, I had to make changes. Then Jenny Craig came along.

In hindsight, I had no idea if it would work or if I would embarrass myself on a scale I didn't want to imagine. But I had to take the risk. I almost had no choice. And once I did, I discovered hope where none had existed before. I also started down the path to where I am today, a better me.

Listening to Obama talk about change made me feel the way I had when I started my diet and couldn't wait for my weekly weigh-in. It hadn't been easy. I had felt the pain of altering my way of life as I confronted the problems, corrected the things that weren't working, and used new muscles. But change had happened before my eyes. As Obama said, it was going to hurt for a while, but we'd get through it.

I knew some people were put off by Obama's ideas, some because they were frightened and others because they disagreed. My dad was among them. But those ideas were the very things that inspired and energized me.

I counted down the days till the November 4 election, which was shaping up to be a big event in our house. Tom's son, Tony, was voting for the first time, and both he and Wolfie suddenly showed interest in politics. As the boys realized the issues were going to affect their lives more than any other in recent times, they paid attention to our dinner table discussions and debates. It was neat to see their eyes opening in a new way.

On election day, I got up early, threw on jeans and a t-shirt, grabbed Tom, and went to our polling place, a nearby fire station. It was the first time we'd voted there. At the old polling place, I used to see friends and familiar faces, people I knew through Wolfie's school or from around the neighborhood. This time I didn't know anyone, but people were friendly and the mood was upbeat and almost festive, making me suspect this was a mostly pro-Obama crowd.

I squeezed Tom's hand as we waited in line and thought what a cool chapter of history we were getting a chance to participate in. I hurried through the rest of my day so I could plant myself in front of the TV and watch the returns. It was like a ten-hour date with Wolf Blitzer. When Wolfie came home from school, he asked if there was any news about the election. I explained that results wouldn't start filtering in until polls closed back East. I invited him to sit next to me and watch.

"I just want to know the winner," he said, shaking his head.

"Yeah, but understanding why that person wins is pretty interesting, too," I said.

"I know," he said. "Call me when there's news."

I let him take two steps toward his bedroom, where he was going to phone his girlfriend.

"There's news," I said.

"Very funny," he called.

But he was more interested than either of us suspected. After checking in with Liv, Wolfie came back out of his bedroom and stood behind the couch, watching the TV and listening as I explained what was going on. He didn't scoff when I told him that we were watching history happen. I felt like patting the cushion next to me on the sofa and inviting him to cuddle up next to me, as I used to do when he was little and interested in a good afternoon snuggle. But I didn't push it.

We seemed to watch in shifts. While I prepared dinner, Tom and the boys sat in front of the TV, shouting updates to me. Later that night, Tom and I were a cozy twosome as the boys played music in their room. By the time Obama made his acceptance speech, though, all of us were together, sharing the moment as a family, talking excitedly about the meaning of the election. I cried.

"I was waiting for the tears," Wolfie said. "We should have made bets on when she would cry."

"Oh, be quiet," I said. "This is cool."

"I know," he said. "It's not something to cry about."

"I'm crying because I'm happy," I said.

"At least you aren't yelling at the TV like you did during the debates."

Tom laughed and then said, "Remember she would yell, 'Damnit, speak back to him! Tell him he's lying.' "

Everyone had a good laugh at my expense. I was happy to admit that Obama was a much better man than I. And now he was president of the United States.

Early the next morning, Tom and I went for a rigorous hike in a nearby canyon, and as I took in the panoramic sweep of the Valley from atop the highest peak, I gushed, "Amazing." I was talking about the view, but I was still filled with emotion from the previous night's election. It didn't matter whether I was at home or out in nature, I still needed to talk about it.

I took a deep breath, wrapped my arm around Tom, and waxed eloquent about Obama, the clear blue sky and sense of hope I got from looking out on the city. Whether I was on top of a hill or at home, I loved a good view. Hey, what's wrong with being able to see great distances? I'll take a vision any day.

When Tom and I started to date, I used to sit at my kitchen table and watch the planes coming in and taking off at Burbank airport, wondering if one of those was Tom's plane. I still look out from home at planes and cars on the freeway with a curiosity about the people going places and the things going on in their lives. I told Tom that I had a sense most of us were celebrating today.

"Not your parents," he said.

"Well, yeah—duh," I said, ignoring the joke. "But I love the way Obama looks at his wife and the way she looks at him. Even better, I like the way they look at their daughters. You can see he—that both of them—want this world to be a better place for their daughters."

"I can dig that," Tom said.

For the next week, I looked for excuses to talk about politics and change. Like everyone else, I had Obama on my mind. I heard someone on a daytime talk show mention that women were having sex dreams about the president-elect. Not me. But I was borderline-obsessed with who he was going to choose for his cabinet and how he was going to tackle the economy, unemployment, the war, and health care.

My excitement reminded me of the way I had felt during the first days after I decided to go on a diet. Although it was way too early to see any results, I knew they were coming. I was full of anticipation and hope.

I keep returning to this idea, this word hope. It's key. As far as I'm concerned, the first and most necessary ingredient for healthy, positive change is hope. Once you have hope, you begin to acquire faith, and with faith comes strength . . . and suddenly you have a whole new thing going.

By the time we went back to Arizona for Thanksgiving, I had moved past my initial enthusiasm about the election. As much as I liked voicing my opinion about politics and current events, I turned my attention to something even nearer and dearer to my heart, namely organizing the holiday dinner. Either I was at the grocery store, talking to my brothers or my sister-in-law Stacy on the phone, or visiting my mom, whose recovery was up and down.

Resting at home, she felt on the mend some days and lacking energy on others. A residence nurse came in three times a week to help her. My mom didn't know whether she would be up to attending dinner, so I was thrilled when my dad called on Thanksgiving morning to say they would be over for dinner

"How's Mom?" I asked.

"A little tired this morning."

"But she's okay?"

"Yes—and looking forward to being with everyone."

Tom and I shared kitchen duties. He made the turkey and I prepared the mashed potatoes and various fixings. Later that night, my brother Pat and his wife Stacy came over with stuffing and sumptuous cheese grits, which I tasted and then immediately declared off-limits to myself since I feared one more bite could cause me to finish the entire pot.

As for dessert, I normally made pecan and pumpkin pies, but this year I opted for store-bought pies, figuring they wouldn't be as much of a temptation. I heard plenty of complaints about that decision, including one from my mom, who spotted them on the counter as soon as she and my dad arrived and said, "Oh, you didn't make your pies?" Suddenly we were debating our all-time favorite desserts. I realized why food was central to every occasion. It brought the family together and provided the opportunity for us to talk about and reflect on and compare notes about our lives.

Early into dinner, my mom's stomach began to hurt. She tried not to make a thing of it, but it persisted and she got tired. You could see the sudden change. Worried, my dad put her jacket on and told the rest of us they were going to head home. He was in a hurry to get her into into bed, as if that were a safe zone where she could get under the covers and wake up feeling better in the morning.

A few days later, though, my mom had to go back into the hospital with a nasty infection in her sternum. I was back in Los Angeles. My dad was calm as he gave me the latest news from her doctor. Even though the doctor had warned such infections were tough and tricky, he told my dad that she would beat it. My dad didn't sound convinced.

I was standing in the kitchen as we talked. I stared at my calendar and started to figure out which appointments I could cancel so I could go back and forth to Arizona. After the call, I looked out the window. A blanket of gray marine fog and clouds obscured my view. I turned on the TV and saw a report about Obama. I had no idea what they were saying. I was thinking about my mom. In my head, I heard myself say, "Yes, we can."

Notes to Myself

I'm glad Tom is up for working out with me. As with life in general, talking to or just having someone by my side makes it a lot more enjoyable.

I craved an ice cream sundae. I was remembering how great the last one I ate tasted. Then I remembered how great it was throwing out my size 12s and 10s and 8s. Suddenly I lost my craving for ice cream.

You don't need a reason to smile—just do it. It doesn't count as exercise, but using the muscles it takes to smile automatically lifts the spirits. And like a yawn, it's contagious.

Will overalls ever come back in style? Why did they go out of style?

Chapter Eighteen

Dexter

On December 4th, my mom returned to the hospital. The next day she underwent surgery and, a week later, another one. Both procedures were related to the infection that had nested in her sternum. I was back East both times and kept my cell phone in my pocket even when I was in front of the camera. Every couple of hours my dad called and gave a detailed update. He clung to the facts as if he were an uncertain swimmer hanging onto an inner tube. I listened to the tone of his voice. The best I can say is that it was a difficult, precarious time.

Four days after her second surgery, my mom was moved to an after-care facility. She needed more specialized medical help than my dad could provide at home even with a part-time nurse. By then I was back home and talking to her throughout the day. She sounded tired and put off by the whole ordeal, as if it were a bother.

She was still pissed off that it had interrupted their cruise. She was also resigned to the plan her doctor had prescribed.

"What else can I do?" she asked.

Nothing. Two surgeries, a week apart, and now an after-care facility. This was new territory for all of us. We kept track of what we had to know, asked for second opinions, made the best decisions possible, and then just let go and let God.

"Just let me know if you need anything," I said. "I'll keep checking in."

After hanging up I turned around and saw my beautiful Abyssinian cat staring at me. I couldn't tell whether Dexter was questioning me or offering comfort. Those gold-green eyes of his were a mystery, but they were rich in thought and intense. And as was usually the case, they were trained on me. If Dexter wasn't lounging in a sun-bathed corner of the house, he was following me. He lurked behind corners and tables, rarely letting me out of his sight.

The other day I ran to get the phone while holding an armload of laundry stacked halfway up my face. Only my eyes peered over the top. Then the phone rang. Thinking it could be my dad with news, I struggled to pick it up without dropping all the clothes. It turned out to be a phone solicitor, a woman who greeted me by asking, "Are you the homeowner?" I was about to unload a few weeks of pent-up frustration and concern on this woman when I felt Dexter rub against my legs. I calmed down.

"No, I'm not the homeowner," I said. "We're not interested and please take me off your list."

With Dexter following me from room to room, I put away the laundry. When I was finished, I picked up Dexter and cradled him in my arms like a baby. He hated being picked up. I suppose I would hate it, too. Then again, there have been plenty of times I had wished God would swoop down, lift me up, rub my tummy, and reassure me that everything was going to be okay. It doesn't work that way, though. Like it or not, even with help from a therapist or, doctor, or inspiration from a sermon, we humans have to pick ourselves up.

A few days later I flew to Arizona. For some stupid reason, I thought back a couple of years to when Dexter had been sick. He'd needed two operations. The second one kept him in the hospital a long time. After a few days, I was able to visit him. The nurse brought him in and put him on the ground. He had a plastic cone around his neck. As soon as he saw me, though, he jumped into my arms. I had to set him back down so I didn't accidentally tear his stitches. But he kept twirling around my legs. He couldn't get close enough to me.

"I wish I knew what he was thinking," I'd said to the nurse.

"He's thinking that he likes seeing you, that he missed you, and he's glad you're here," she said.

My mom was glad to see me when I visited her, though she wasn't nearly as relieved as I was to see her. I tried to hide my emotions. My mom was not well. Maybe she was on the road to recovery, but I didn't see it. If she was, it was a bumpy road. Pale and weak, she had a bunch of tubes in her, and she had to wear a vest to keep her chest tight and the drains in place. Despite the upsetting picture, though, there was good news. She wasn't dying. I wasn't going to lose my mom, as I'd feared deep down so many times during this ordeal.

I set down a little present I had brought and looked at my dad, my mother's knight in shining armor since the start of this ordeal on the cruise ship. I was so proud of him that I forgave every single one of his right-wing opinions. But I didn't actually say that out loud. I wanted to reserve the right to get pissed off at him sometime in the future if I needed to.

Knowing they had been cooped up in this room for too long, I talked as if we hadn't seen each other for years. I let information spill out of me. I wanted to inject some energy into their lives. I appreciated the life they had together, the fact they had been married more than fifty years and had arrived at their seventies with a zest for adventure that matched the practicality they had employed while raising their family. They'd done good, and I wanted that to continue.

The damnedest thing was, I had a better relationship with my mom now than at any time in the past. Maybe that wasn't unusual as people age and mellow, though I don't think either of us had mellowed. But we definitely had an easier and more enjoyable time with each other. I had learned to avoid the little things that led to fights and irritability, and she no doubt had learned a few tricks when dealing with me. We had grown into each other.

Despite our often differing opinions, the two of us agreed that we had learned to be kinder and more loving to each other because we were kinder and more loving to ourselves. We hadn't simply lost weight running on the treadmill or pedaling the exercise bike, as my mom had done. We had also gotten rid of some of the crap from the past that had made conversations and time spent together needlessly tense. As a result, we were able to appreciate each other.

Thankfully we had arrived at that place before my mom got sick and didn't have to confront any past issues while she was lying in bed at the after-care facility, which she hated. As good as the facility was, she was depressed from being there. I didn't blame her. It was depressing to be around extremely sick people, many of who, as she noted, would never leave. She couldn't avoid thinking she was one of them.

At the same time, I reassured her that she wasn't among the sickest and needed to keep up a positive attitude. My brother, Pat, and his wife, Stacy, did the same. We urged her to remember that her doctor had promised she would go home soon.

I admired the way my dad was holding up. He spent every night with my mom, sleeping on a chair that folded out into a bed. I came every afternoon for ten days. We talked about the news, looked at magazines, reminisced about car trips we had taken forty years earlier, and laughed. I wondered why the heck I had wasted time wishing my folks had behaved one way or another rather than appreciating the thousands of coincidences, miracles, and hours of worry and hard work that had needed to happen in their lives for them to produce five children, raise four, deal with the death of one, and survive another forty-eight years.

Did it really matter that our politics differed? No. Did it still matter that we'd had a tough time when I was a teenager? No. Despite all the misunderstandings and hurt feelings over the years, we had arrived at the present in fairly good working order, and we were continuing to improve. At various times each of us had done a sort of spring cleaning of unnecessary emotional crap and clutter. We had gotten rid of the gripes that no longer mattered. We had let go, and let love take over.

One day I walked into my mom's room flustered and upset. I had been caught in a speed trap on one of the long straightaways outside of Phoenix. The speed limit was 65 mph. I had set my cruise control for 68. Suddenly a 55 mph sign appeared out of nowhere, I saw the flash of an automated camera taking my picture, which meant a speeding ticket would soon show up in the mail. I was pissed.

My parents laughed as I cursed Phoenix Sheriff Joe Arpaio and swore I wasn't going to pay the fine. Seeing them distracted by my temper tantrum, though, may have been worth the couple of hundred bucks the fine would cost me.

Another day I reminded my mom that I had committed to try to get into a bikini for a new Jenny Craig commercial. I emphasized the word "try." She teased me for being typically noncommittal. I would have been ticked off by that comment a few years earlier. Now I knew she was right. She even made me laugh when she said, "If you don't do it, maybe I will."

"I'll let them know," I said.

As the days rolled by, we faced another family issue: what to do about Christmas. With my mom in the after-care facility, it was complicated. Tom's children were spending the holiday with us in L.A., and I needed to get home to prepare. Pat and Stacy also had plans. But we were game to change everything and celebrate the holiday with my parents. Except that my mom vetoed such thoughts, declaring, "I'm not having Christmas in this godforsaken place. I'm not celebrating until I'm home."

I argued briefly before realizing that my mom was using this as motivation to get her butt out of the after-care facility. I didn't want to get in the way of anything that put her in a positive frame of mind. Nor did Pat and Stacy, who nonetheless filled her room with Christmas decorations, including a tree and lights, poinsettias, candies, and other fun goodies. They made it look like Santa's workshop.

I returned to Los Angeles and a house full of kids. I felt rushed; everything was last minute. Plus Wolfie asked me to make this

Christmas "really cool" since it was his last one before turning eighteen.

"And then what happens?" I asked.

"I'll be an adult," he said.

"So."

"I probably won't believe in Santa."

"That's your problem," I said.

"Ma! Can't we just make it cool this year?"

"Fine," I said. "Let's make it a really cool Christmas. The coolest ever."

It may have been among the best. On Christmas Eve, we bought a tree and spent the night decorating it, playing games, and drinking hot chocolate. Around eleven, Tom and I tucked Dominic into bed, said goodnight to the girls, and told Wolfie and Tony not to play their music too loud lest they frighten Santa's reindeer from landing on the roof.

I was exhausted when Tom and I finally got into bed. It was a good tired, though. I felt like I had done my best to make everyone happy and the holiday a good one. Only one thing was missing. Then, a few minutes later, Dexter jumped on the bed and fixed himself a comfy spot at my feet. Before I closed my eyes, I glanced at the clock. It was just after midnight. Merry Christmas.

Notes to Myself

Pick up some new sports bras that don't give me uni-boob. And while at the mall, bypass the food court, even if you smell the free samples.

It's not "No." It's more like "Eat ya later."

Keep your eye on the goal—healthy living. Happy living will follow.

I know it's easy to get stuck in a routine, and that probably explains why I've felt in a rut lately. So today I'm going to step out of my comfort zone. I'll let Tom pick the movie we're going to watch. (He's tired of chick flicks.)

Chapter Nineteen

Day Pass

On the day after Christmas, we packed up the car with kids and clothes and drove to Arizona. My poor dad was busier than ever dividing his time between my mom in the after-care facility and their home, which needed a certain amount of tending to even though neither of them was there. He half-jokingly reminded us that he had supervised the construction of automobile plants, so he was able to handle feeding the cat, bringing in the mail, and making sure the sprinklers went on.

His hardest task was dealing with my mom. She was sitting up in bed when I finally saw her again. The first thing I noticed was her voice. It was back to normal even if the rest of her wasn't.

"Do you want a Starburst?" she asked, pointing to a large bag of the candy on her night table. "I don't know why, but I have had the strongest craving for them."

"I guess so," I said, looking at the bag.

"Your dad went to the market and bought me a pile of them," she said with a shrug.

I looked at the package.

"Geez, 20 calories in each piece?" I said.

She waved me off.

"Don't be a spoilsport. I don't have much else going for me here."

"Hey, live it up," I said, holding up my hands as if I was backing off.

Despite all the visits from her children, I could see that my mom was suffering from being at the after-care facility. It was taking a toll mentally and I worried that it was also affecting the speed with which she was healing physically. It was a difficult situation. She knew she was sick and needed special care, but she didn't think like a sick person. She wanted to smell the crisp winter air and walk through her neighborhood, not the antiseptic corridors of the facility.

Even though she was supposedly getting better, she had a hard time believing she would actually leave. She complained that being cooped up in the facility was robbing her of her brain. Worse, it was eroding her spirit. She pointed out other patients and detailed their ailments as if she didn't want to catch what they had.

"That woman there," she said, gesturing to a spindle of a woman in a pale blue night gown. "She's 101 years old."

"Wow," I said.

"She's never leaving here. So what good is it being that old?"

"Mom!" I scolded.

"It's true," she said. "And that old man you saw scooting around in a wheelchair."

"Yeah."

"Cancer. He's never getting out of here either."

"Mother, please."

"And every time I want to watch shows on the good TV in the living room, the same old woman is sleeping in the chair. She's in her nineties. She's always there. Daytime. Nighttime."

"Poor thing," I said.

"She has her own room, too," my mom said. "She probably doesn't want to go there because she knows she's never leaving here, either."

Finally, I had had enough. I told her to get over her negativity and tried to put her in a better frame of mind, reluctantly lecturing her on the importance of a positive attitude. The mind has incredible sway over the body. If you're depressed, your body will reflect it one unhealthy way or another. But as I told my mom, if you think positively and visualize yourself healthier, you will find a way to get yourself in that same kind of shape.

"If you think you're never going to get out of here, you won't," I said. "But if you focus on sitting in your favorite chair and watching HGTV at home, with all of us around you, you'll find a way to get there."

"I don't know," she said.

"Focus on the next cruise you're going to take," I said.

"Well, the doctor—"

"Come on, Mom," I interrupted.

"We're never going on a cruise again," my dad chimed. "You don't know what we've been through."

"Both of you, stop it!" I implored. "I know this has been hellish. But the worst of it is over. It's all up from here."

• • •

I want to think my talk had an impact on them. I don't know for sure if it did. But the following afternoon when I walked into my mom's room, I found both of them in much better spirits. My dad had spoken to my mom's doctor and wrangled her a day pass. She could go home.

"Isn't it great?" she said. "I couldn't believe it when Andy asked, and they said yes."

"See what I mean," I said.

On January 1, my mom went home for the day and the first thing she did was take a good hot bath. She came out of the bathroom slowly, but obviously refreshed, and declared, "I finally feel clean." I took that to mean she finally felt like she would get better. She had washed the icky veneer of sickness off her. Then she went in her bedroom and ran her fingers over the clothes in her closet.

"I just wanted to smell them," she said. "It's been so long since I was able to wear anything but a hospital gown."

At her request, we celebrated Christmas. Since she had waited this long and we knew it was momentous for her, we pulled out all the stops. That afternoon, Tom and I and Wolfie, and my brother Pat and his wife, Stacy, met at my parents' house, carrying in food and gifts and decorations. Within an hour, you would have sworn we had turned back the clock six days to Christmas.

My mom took it all in from her leather chair, occasionally turning to watch her favorite HGTV shows. We didn't let her lift a finger. We teased her about being on a day pass, as if she were on probation. If she didn't listen to us about taking it easy, we joked that she would have to go back for even longer. My dad also made sure that she resisted the urge to get up and help.

During dinner, my brother and I reminisced about how special Christmas had always been in our family, especially when we lived in Delaware. On Christmas Eve, my mom would put us to bed early while my dad went out and bought a tree. Then he and my mom stayed up all night decorating it and putting out presents.

"Wait a minute," Wolfie said, looking upset.

"What?"

"Are you saying there's no Santa Claus?"

I punched him in the arm. I wanted to keep talking about my memories of waking up in the morning and finding the gorgeous tree surrounded by presents and the mouth-watering smells coming out of the kitchen.

On one of those mornings, I found a blue box of Barbie dolls under the tree. I still have the box, with Barbie inside, as well as all the beautiful clothes my mom made for her. It sits on the top shelf of my closet. I probably haven't played with them for forty years. Nor can I remember the last time I opened the box. But I can't imagine not having them.

As I described some of the doll clothes I used to love, including a black-and-white bathing suit, Wolfie rolled his eyes. So did Tom. I didn't understand why they couldn't tolerate me waxing nostalgic about some adorable ice-skating outfits and formal gowns. I've sat through countless stories about my son's bass and my boyfriend's childhood athletic feats. What was the big deal?

"The difference is you love football," Tom said. "I don't love Barbies."

The point was moot. Before we got to dessert, my mom began to fade and my dad shooed all of us out of the house so he could put her to bed. On the way out, I told my mom that I hoped she'd liked her presents. It was such a trivial thing to say, but it was Christmas, even if it was a week later.

"Being home was my gift," she said. "It was the best medicine."

"And as I told you the other day, it's only going to go up from here," I said.

"I hope you're right."

"I know I am."

As it turned out, I was. My mom returned to the after-care facility and spent twelve more days there before being discharged. She wasn't in perfect health when she got out, but she was on her way to making the full recovery her doctors had promised her was possible.

Much of that recovery would be in her own hands, just as making the turn in my life had been up to me. If you get your head into a different place, the rest of you will follow. The message applies whether you are beginning a diet, recovering from an illness, or figuring out what to do after being laid off from a job.

Change is a process; the key is to start. Obviously you can't remake your life in a single day, but you have to begin someplace. It's like giving yourself a day pass, the same kind my mom's doctor gave her. And it's not hard. You simply step out of your own way for a few hours. You put yourself in a different head space. You change environments And you tune in to your inner voice, the voice that tells you who you really want to be, and then you become that person. You visualize yourself in that role.

Try it for a day. Then spend the rest of the week figuring out how to be that person two days in a row, then three, and so on.

I had done exactly that before committing to Jenny Craig. I

spent the day with Kirstie Alley, who had gone on the diet before me. She told me about the diet, let me try the food, and worked out with me. That whole day I was with her, I tried to envision whether I could be that person who could stick to the program. I left her house thinking that I could—and soon I was.

For all my cheerleading, I went home feeling like a bit of a hypocrite and worse, knowing I had strayed a little too much from my diet and workout. My brother and sister-in-law's gumbo was to blame. Before we left Arizona, they had whipped up a batch, which is actually enough to feed four to five families, and I had indulged too much. Aside from the fact that it was delicious, I ate because I was stressed-out from dealing with my parents.

I beat myself up for the slip, and I guess I was still moping around when my trainer came over. Christopher Lane and I were still getting to know each other. Blond and blue-eyed, he's the guy Jillian had called to help get me into bikini shape. She had injected him into my life like a shot of vitamin B12. The first time he came to the house I thought, Well, isn't he a handsome fellow. The next time I was more like, Oh, my God, what did I get myself into?

I will describe Christopher in more detail in a bit. Let me just say that, by this time, he knew me well enough to notice that I was walking around with my shoulders slumped. I hemmed and hawed when he asked if I had kept up my workout in Arizona. Finally, I confessed about the gumbo.

"Forget about it," he said. "Today's a new day. I want you to have your gumbo. Jenny wants you to have your gumbo. I've heard about your gumbo. I want to try your gumbo."

Before he took his jacket off, he put me on the treadmill and told me about a woman he had trained for almost two years. At her insistence, he also had to train her overweight Golden Retriever.

"Really?" I asked, wondering if he had put the dog on the treadmill the way he had just done with me.

He shrugged.

"After six months, the woman was the same weight. But her Golden Retriever had lost 10 pounds."

I didn't know whether he was telling the truth, but I laughed. He continued to tell stories and before realizing it, I had been jogging for twelve minutes. I had let go of the fact that I hadn't worked out in Arizona as much as I had planned and began charting new goals with Christopher. He had me thinking about how well I was doing in that very moment. He commented on my strong pace and talked about the exercises we were going to do outside. He said he had a new routine for later in the week. At some point, he had me acknowledge that I was looking forward, not stuck in the past.

"Everyone has a bad day," he said. "They slip or they don't work out. It's okay. You have to allow yourself. Let yourself have a day when you eat or don't work out. Then get to the gym the next day. Don't punish yourself for getting off track."

"Why?" I laughed. "That's what I do."

"I know you're joking," he said.

"Half-joking," I shrugged. "I'm trying."

"That's all you have to do," he said. "If you're eating poorly or not working out, don't let it become one of those things where you say, I'll start again next week. You want to start the next day. If you're driving down the road and you blow out a tire, you don't get out of your car and shoot the other tires out. You fix the tire and you keep going to your destination."

"Just where is my destination?" I asked, glancing at the readout on the treatmill.

"Where do you think?" he replied.

"Getting my ass in a bikini."

He smiled.

"Okay, I'll keep running. But tell me when I get there."

"That's funny," he said.

"Why?"

"Because I won't know. You'll tell me."

Notes to Myself

✤

One of the best moves I made was moving the exercise routine outside. A brisk walk through a new neighborhood, a jog on the beach, a hike up a mountain. I enjoyed breathing fresh air and had the sense of actually going someplace rather than climbing stairs to nowhere.

Went out to dinner two nights in a row and avoided bread and potatoes, butter, and dessert. I had fish and vegetables. I was impressed with how good I could feel by avoiding filler. I think I'll try it in other areas of my life.

There are food groups for a reason. I've always been in the group that likes to eat.

I've been telling myself that I need to come from a place of inner peace—not a place of wanting an extra piece. And you know what? I'm doing much better in that department.

Chapter Twenty

Running

In the middle of January, I ran almost 3.2 miles through my neighborhood, a new personal best. Tom was nowhere to be seen. Though we had started out together, I had left him somewhere around the two-mile mark. I found him on my way back, his male ego dangling by a thread as I coasted up alongside.

"Go ahead and make fun of me," he said. "I deserve it."

"I'm not going to tease you," I said. "I just want to know if you are going to be able to make it back home. Or do you want to wait here while I run back and get the car?"

A little bit of a show-off, I got a laugh out of Christopher, who had been running alongside me. At this point, we were a tightly-knit threesome. Christopher and I worked out daily, and Tom joined us most of the time. He was getting noticeably buff and seeing results much more quickly than I was, even though I had gone on-record about getting in a bikini to those involved in my life and career.

Now that I was past the holidays and my mom was on the rebound, I had gotten serious about my workouts. The fact that I was running was enough of an indication that I was making the mental adjustments I needed to take my fitness to the next level. But the real turning point was the day I met Christopher. Jillian took care of all the arrangements, so that one day he showed up at my house. As I said, he was blond and cute and had eyes the color of turquoise jewelry. I thought those assets would make it easy for me to do sit-ups while he was holding my ankles.

I also really liked that Christopher has a normal-looking physique, not one of those over-pumped, steroid-infused bodies you see in Hollywood gyms. Don't get me wrong; he is taut and in enviable shape. But his buffness seemed accessible, the male version of what I was going for (sort of). He had been a diver in college and has a few graduate degrees. The man knows his stuff.

Within minutes of meeting me, he had me on the treadmill. It was only after I had broken a sweat that I began to find out about his background. He later told me that that had been the point. He didn't lay out a plan as much as he got me going. Only after he had me walking at a brisk pace did he start to ask questions about my general health, whether I took medication, how my knees and ankles were, and so on.

"Do you ice your knees after running?" he had asked.

"No."

"Why?"

"Because I don't run."

"You will soon enough—and you'll ice your knees afterward."

I shook my head. I told him flat-out that I would do anything other than run. I wasn't a runner. I hated running. I didn't have the long, sinewy body of a runner. I wasn't light on my feet. I might have tried joking that the only time I ran was mealtime, but Christopher didn't crack a smile.

"You're going to run," he said.

This became a persistent theme through the holidays. Christopher knew that I was distracted and not yet ready to make a serious commitment. I had too much on my plate, literally and figuratively. But upon reconnecting in mid-January, he brought up the running again. He was adamant about it, too. Just as I was, in my determination not to run. I felt pushed at the pace he had me going on the treadmill, a fast walk.

"I've heard you loud and clear, telling me that you're not a runner," he said.

"I'm not."

"Well, I'm still going to turn you into a runner," he said.

"You don't understand what I'm saying," I said.

"No, you don't understand," he said. "There's no way to succeed in this process if I don't get you running."

We may have sounded contentious, but we weren't. I laughed more than I probably should have as Christopher pushed me into new territory. It helped to have Tom around to make fun of. Tom is a natural athlete, but back then in terms of running, he was more a sprinter than a distance man. As Christopher started us out, we were like the tortoise and the hare. I loved passing him. I don't know why—I'm sure it's related to having grown up with three brothers—but I got the biggest kick out of looking over my shoulder and saying, "See ya!"

Mind you, after I gave in to Christopher about running, he came over the next day and said he was going to teach me how to run. Teach me how to run? Although I had said I wasn't a runner,

I knew how to run. Who doesn't know how to run? You walk real fast, and then faster, until you are running.

I had been running with my brothers since I played my first game of touch football. As a teenager, I had been a stud on the *Battle of the Network Stars* TV special. I had video as proof. It was me and Kristy McNichol going neck and neck in the sprints. I still roused Tom and the boys into an annual touch football game at the beach. I knew how to frickin' run.

I don't mean to drone on, but this was like being told I didn't know how to pray. Although I had limited knowledge about the rituals and beliefs of different religions, I suspect that most people, when praying to God, or whatever they call their Higher Power, say basically the same thing: "Hello, God, I know you're busy. But if you have time and an extra miracle, I want to thank you for my day, and maybe ask a favor . . ."

While I may be right about prayer, boy, did I learn that I was wrong about running. Christopher explained that while I did know how to run fast over a short distance, I didn't know how to do it over a long haul. As soon as he said that, bells went off in my head. He may as well have been describing the problem faced by 95 percent of everyone who has ever gone on a diet and then re-gained weight, including me: We knew how to lose weight. But we didn't know how to keep it off over the long distance, over the rest of our lives. Wasn't that what this was all about, anyway, what I was trying to figure out about maintenance? It's part of what I'd been looking to find.

Christopher started me out slowly, at a speed that was equivalent to about 4.2 miles per hour. I was still walking, just incrementally faster than I had been going on the treadmill. He explained that getting fit was a process—an "evolution" was how he put it—and he was planting seeds that he could build on. First a fast walk, then a slow run, and then who knew what was next. His goal was to give me as much as I could do, then push me a little more.

"Oh God," I groaned.

"Don't worry," he said.

"Tell me that when I'm icing my knees," I laughed.

One day he came over and said we were going for a run around the neighborhood. We didn't go far, maybe a mile. About two blocks into it, he stopped me and explained that running outdoors was different from running on a treadmill, as if I wasn't already able to make that comparison. I was panting hard.

"You're going too fast," he said.

"This sounds like the discussion we had two weeks ago," I said. "I'm running."

"But you don't have to do it like you're trying out for the Olympics," he said. "There's no one chasing you. You aren't trying to get away from anyone."

He reiterated that running was about consistency and endurance, not speed. By this time, with our daily workouts, he had said this to me so often that I realized it wasn't because I was dumb or didn't get it. It was because I needed the reminder. Repetition wasn't necessary; it was essential. He also corrected my posture and taught me to breathe in every couple of steps and then exhale over the same number. And he reminded me to be patient with myself.

"It's a slow build," he said. "You don't get results overnight."

I understood. I don't know what clicked, but one day after Christopher left, I started to laugh. This whole bit about running suddenly struck me as ironic. As I later told Tom, I had been running my whole life. Not in the way Christopher had me running. I had been running away from things. I had been avoiding the issues that had come to define and then take over my life. And when you run like that, you have no idea where you are going. It's painful.

But now I was running toward something. I had an actual goal. I felt much better about everything. I actually looked forward to pushing myself every day to get stronger. I even began to look forward to running with Christopher.

Besides my getting in better shape, Christopher promised that I would be able to decide what I wanted my body to look like. No one had ever said that to me. Nor had I ever thought about changing any part of my body other than my weight. For that reason alone, I had always shied away from strapless gowns and tank tops, two styles I would have loved to wear on numerous occasions. But I didn't like my arms.

"You're serious?" I asked.

He nodded.

"In that case, I'd like to be five-seven, long, and slender," I said.

"Within reason."

"Then don't make promises you can't keep," I said with a grin as I huffed and puffed.

"We'll get to a point where you can tell me you want a line here or you want this gone or a curve there."

I slapped my rear end.

"Right here," I said. "Make it smaller. I have to fit into a bikini by March."

"I know," he said, laughing. "I may have heard that before."

To be clear, Christopher explained that he couldn't train me and focus only on my butt. It wasn't going to work. He warned that I would probably lose weight and see more definition every-where except my butt because my body would try to hang on to its shape there. It would be the last place where we would see change.

Speaking of weight, at that time, I weighed between 131 and 133 depending on the day. I decided that 132 pounds was where I would plant my stake. If I got any higher, I had to sound the alarm and get down. But I figured that in order to feel good about seeing myself in a bikini on film, I needed to get down into the neighbor-hood of 125 to 122 pounds. Christopher assured me that I could do it.

Soon he was talking to me about increasing my metabolism, something I had always assumed was slow and set. But now, he wanted to "get my burn rate up," as he put it. According to him, my basal metabolic rate—or BMR—was about 1,300, meaning my body burned that many calories per day just by being alive. He wanted to raise that number at least 10 percent, making my body even more efficient at burning calories. Through exercise, he planned to get me to the point where on some days I would be burning upwards of 3,500 calories.

"In one day?" I asked.

"Yep," he said.

"I'm going to be able to eat anything I want."

"No, you aren't," he said. "In fact, I want you looking even more carefully at what you're putting into your body."

"I eat well," I said.

"I know. I've seen the commercials," he said, smiling. "But I want you drinking more water. And when you want to have that extra glass of wine, I want you to consider that it's going to negate half of our workout session. So you'll have to ask yourself whether that extra glass is worth it."

"Kind of strict, don't you think?"

"You're in training," he said. "Right?"

I was, indeed. As proof, our workouts grew more intense. Christopher showed up mid-morning, after I'd had my coffee and worked on the crossword. We ran through the neighborhood, working up from one mile to two, then three. I thought I was going to die. We also did sit-ups, push-ups, and step-ups on the coffee table or some other piece of furniture indoors or outdoors, depending on the weather. He didn't use much equipment; my body weight supplied the resistance, and boy, did it try to resist.

He changed our routines regularly so I wouldn't get bored, but we always ran. I couldn't believe it. I didn't. Let me say this: As much as I ran and would continue to run for months, I hated every single step. It never became easy for me. But I liked the mechanics of putting one foot in front of the other and carrying my own weight. I liked the runner's high I got after about twenty minutes. Most of all, I liked the satisfaction I got from achieving a goal every day.

There was something profound about the way I had relearned this most basic activity and rethought its significance. It symbolized all the other things in my life that I had either relearned or was in the process of relearning, including how to eat, how to choose my words carefully when in an argument, how to exercise patience, how to forgive, and how to appreciate the little things in life.

I was also re-envisioning my life in terms of who I was and who I wanted to be. I now saw it as a process, like running, something I worked at in little, achievable increments every day.

On January 20, the day Obama was sworn into office, I completed my first Elevado, a four-and-a-half mile run along a neighborhood street of that name in Beverly Hills. It was a favorite run of Christopher's, one he liked because it was super pretty and a fairly significant distance. I have to be honest: when he said it was about four-and-a-half miles, I thought "no way," even though we had been training for it.

Once we began, though, I focused on getting to the halfway point. That's all I thought about. I just wanted to know how much farther I had to go. After we turned around, I counted the steps back. As Christopher had said, it was all mental—as is much of life. Indeed, at the end, I couldn't believe I had run 4.2 miles straight, without stopping.

"Well, believe it, baby," he said. "And ice those knees."

I couldn't believe it, but I started to feel like an athlete. Less than two weeks later, I met Christopher at the beach and we went for a run. I worked through the first twenty minutes, then felt my endorphins kick in, and suddenly I was, dare I say, enjoying myself. Christopher and I traded advice about our relationships as we ran. Gradually, though, I stopped talking and concentrated on my breathing. Christopher wondered if I was sick of listening to him talk. No, I said, I wanted to concentrate.

"I'm enjoying my runner's high," I said.

"Oh, now you're a runner," he laughed.

I would never say that. But at the end, Christopher said we had gone 5½ miles. He also said that it was the first time he had seen definition in my legs. Really? The next morning I put on tight athletic shorts and wore them the whole day. My body was starting to change and I wanted to see it.

Notes to Myself

What's wrong with me that I heard someone say, "May all living things be happy and free," and my first thought was, "And may all edible things come with a side of butter."

I took Dexter to the vet, ran home for a meeting, then out to a fitting and back to change for dinner, and I was so insane about getting everyplace on time that I simply sat down and gave myself a time-out. We are always going, going, going. It's important to stop and take a breath and see where you are.

Remember to get the right amount of nutrients every day, including hugs and kisses.

Heard a line by comic Stephen Wright: "If you got everything you wanted, where would you put it?" Good question.

Chapter Twenty-one

T.M.I.

It was February, and I was getting firmer and stronger. I could feel it and sort of see it. I could almost imagine walking around the house without any clothes, but since I never knew when Wolfie or Tony would barrel through, I kept them on. Sorry, Tom. I did make one concession to a better body image. I wore more shorts and tanks.

It was time. After nearly two years of dieting, maintenance, and workouts, I was enjoying my body—kind of. I would never go so far as to say I was ready to declare myself "hot," but we were in a much better relationship. Whether my body was bikini-ready was another matter. As far as I was concerned, it wasn't.

I was stuck. I weighed about 130. One day I would weigh 130.6, another day it would be 131.2. This went on for weeks. I'm not a complainer, but I openly vented my frustration at not being able to break into the 120s. I was working my ass off and not making the progress I wanted. Christopher showed superhuman restraint for not telling me to shut up. He assured me that I would get to where I was supposed to be.

One day, though, following a workout, Tom heard me carping about my weight and said, "I am so sick of these 130s." I whipped around from the kitchen counter where I was preparing an ice bag and looked at him with daggers. Laughing nervously, Christopher said, "Oh no, Tom, don't say that!"

Poor Tom. He knew he had put his foot in his mouth. He was horrified.

"I don't mean you're not going to see the 120s," he said. "I'm just as sick of the 130s as you are. You're going to get there, honey. And I'll be so happy for you."

For a moment, I wondered if I was too obsessed by a number that might not be achievable. I was adamant about not putting myself in a place that was unnatural, unhealthy, or unattainable. Why did I have to have a perfect body? Who had a perfect body anyway? Michelle Pfeiffer was one of the most naturally gorgeous, perfect-looking women I have ever seen, and she was once asked what she would do if she could be anonymous for a day. She said that she would take her children to the beach and enjoy herself without worrying about paparazzi photographing her.

If Michelle Pfeiffer worried about being photographed on the beach in a bathing suit, I had to adjust my expectations. I still felt the sting of being ambushed by paparazzi on the beach two summers earlier. I had weighed 140-something, which was a hell of a lot better than 175. If it happened now? I'm not going to kid anyone. I do not want a telephoto lens aimed at me, ever. I will never be comfortable on a public beach until long-lens cameras are banned. But I feel much better about walking around in shorts.

I began to look at my struggle to break into the 120s as a reality check. I had to be realistic and avoid idealizing a perfect me. Nothing was perfect—unless it was topped with nuts, whipped cream, and a cherry. So I told myself that, when I got into a bikini, if I did, I was going to have to be okay with a little muffin top and still feel proud of my accomplishment.

The day-to-day reality was another thing. Despite the pep talks I gave myself, I wasn't as together or enlightened as I wanted Wolfie or Tom to think. Yes, I'd lost a lot of weight, improved my life in numerous ways, gotten rid of some personal baggage, and acquired some wisdom. I now truly believed that God would love me as much at 180 pounds as He would at 126 pounds. But that wasn't the point. It was going to be my ass in that bikini, and I didn't want to see too much of it.

"Why am I not making more progress?" I asked Christopher one day as he put me through my warm-up exercises.

He reminded me that my body was going to try to fight me, as he'd said at the start of our sessions. He also said that all the traveling that I had done over the past two months had slowed me down. It was hard to make the kind of progress I wanted while eating room service and working out in hotel gyms. To break into the 120s, he said, we were going to have to step it up.

"We're going to work harder?" I winced.

He nodded.

"Oh, crap," I said.

He doubled the ten thousand steps I walked each day above and beyond my workouts to twenty thousand steps. He also created a specific, strict workout for me to follow when I was on the road, and he followed up with e-mails. On my end, I got stricter about my workouts and diet when I was on the road. Without making a big deal out of it, I recommitted myself to the type of discipline I knew was necessary.

"I can see the change in you," Christopher said one day.

"I don't know what it is," I said. "It's like a reaffirmation. Maybe I just believe in myself a little bit more."

"Exactly," he said. "You've always believed. But every day your sense of belief is getting a little stronger."

He was right. Beyond any physical transformation, I was going through a test of faith and belief that was personal and was about my embrace of a Higher Power. God knows, I did enough praying to get through my workouts. If I could get into a bikini and feel comfortable about it, it might be proof that He did exist.

At times when I was working out, I felt like I was on a mission from God, though I felt more affiliated with *Ghostbusters* than any organized religion. As I said, I did a lot of communicating with the Big Guy Upstairs, my favorite being, "Please God, let me run for three more minutes without collapsing."

In fact, I did a lot of counting as I ran (just five more steps, three more, okay, ten more steps and then it'll be easier) and playing of songs on my iPod (I would try to get through one song, then try for two more). I kept an eye on my watch, waiting for my endorphin rush after twenty minutes. I thought about calories I burned. Sometimes my head was so full of numbers I felt like Rain Man.

When I thought I couldn't take any more facts or figures, Christopher came over with a buddy named Rick, who gave me a gadget called a Body Bugg. It was a computerized calorie counter about the size of a digital watch attached to a Velcro band. Rick strapped it around my bicep and explained that it would track how many calories burned through exercise and daily activities as well as how many calories I consumed. At the end of each day, I could see where I stood.

All I had to do was input the food I ate and then download the information from the Body Bugg onto my laptop. I had no problem understanding, but Rick had problems setting up my computer because the Internet was down. It had rained the day before and, as I explained, we always lost service for about twenty-four hours afterward.

"That's the reality of my glamorous life," I said. "The pool leaks, the back patio is falling apart, and our Internet has a mind of its own."

"Too much information," Tom said.

"Well, that's how I am," I shrugged. "You want me, you get the whole package, including the house that is falling apart."

Anyway, it took a few days for me to get used to wearing the Bugg on my arm every day. As an accessory, it didn't go with jeans and T-shirts or with the fancier outfits I occasionally slipped into at night for events. But I kept it on nearly all the time. I also had to record everything I ate and drank—and I mean everything. I had to be exact in order for the Bugg to spit out accurate results.

I didn't realize how much I overlooked or forgot about until I made the effort to be rigorously precise. Christopher had told me that some of his clients had worn the Bugg but lied about what they ate. What was the point? They were only cheating themselves. I believed in the old cliché about being as sick at your secrets. It applied to drugs, alcohol, sex, relationships, and, yes, food.

One thing about me, though: I didn't lie. I had lost weight by being honest about what I ate and how much I exercised, and unlike the majority of people who shed pounds on diets, I had kept it off for a year by applying the same honesty to the rest of my life. Was I perfect? Not by a long shot. But just walking around with fewer secrets gave me the lightness of being that I had craved, that I knew could only be measured in my soul, not on any scale.

For all my trustworthiness, though, I still had second thoughts when Christopher asked for the password to my Body Bugg account. It may have been the idea of giving anyone one of my passwords. I wondered why he wanted it. It was like giving someone permission to look through your window whenever he wanted, day or night. I also asked myself, Didn't he trust me?

No, that wasn't it. As Christopher explained, I was doing an amazing job of working out and staying on top of my meals. But it wasn't good enough. My life was more complicated than normal because of all the traveling I did. He wanted to see everything in black and white each day. He thought it would help me, too.

"You're great at the weight you are right now," he said. "One hundred-thirty is terrific. Don't you feel good?"

"Yes, I do," I said.

"But if you want to go to another level, you have to be amazing."

"I need to be amazing—at least for the day we take pictures."

From then on, I felt as though I had an extra set of eyes on me at all times—and I did: they were Christopher's.

But I also got into it. I inputted info and downloaded computations five or six times a day. Whenever I wanted to know where my calorie deficit stood, or if I had one that particular day, I could see it in black and white. It eliminated the balancing act that every dieter knows too well. There was no more bargaining, tallying, guesswork, or emotion. The numbers simply popped up in front of my face. I was either over, even, or under.

Tom was ecstatic. He no longer had to listen to me go on about what I had eaten that day in what had become a nighttime ritual. He got to kick back. In fact, he took advantage of the situation. Aware that I couldn't resist adding to my daily calorie burn, he began suggesting late-night mattress aerobics.

"Who knows how many more calories you could burn?"

"Hey, great idea!" I smiled.

I liked the Bugg more than I had imagined and wondered what it would be like if such a device could be applied to life in general. In what ways would my life have been different if, at the end of every day, I'd received a printout not just of calories but of my behavior toward myself and other people? What if everyone was held more accountable for his or her actions?

In a sense, it was like asking how you would behave if Jesus were standing next to you. On the other hand, it made me realize that the highest moral authority any of us must answer to at the end of the day is one's self.

I'm a news junkie, and I thought about this idea of accountability more and more as Obama dealt with one crisis after another. Whether he was tackling the financial mess, addressing exorbitant bonuses paid to executives of failing businesses, or closing Guantánamo and putting an end to torture and secret prisons, he seemed to make decisions as if he and America had to answer to a higher authority.

Good for him—and us. What had happened to the country, that we woke up almost daily to headlines about Wall Street cheaters, ballplayers taking steroids, power-drunk politicians, and trashy TV and celebrity websites, that—as we all know—pander to the worst tastes and sensibilities?

Excuse me for getting a little preachy, but we seemed to have lost our moral compass and sense of accountability. It was as if, as a country, we had decided we could eat and drink anything, and not exercise, and then were shocked when we woke up one day fat and unhealthy. I liked to think that Obama was putting America on a diet, teaching people to count calories and make healthier choices. No wonder Rush had a problem with him.

I was a good example of someone who wished that she had been held more accountable in the past, but who had woken up to the truth, made changes, and was on the road to being healther and happier. I'm obviously being overly simplistic when I compare my own transformation to the mind-boggling efforts of leading the country out of complex piles of doo-doo, but, hey, I'm also a good example that change is possible.

I had to continue to believe because, with about one month to go before my bikini shoot, I still hadn't dipped below 130 pounds. I couldn't work any harder. It simply required an enormous effort. One day, I burned more than 3,000 calories, a record for me. The next morning, Christopher was all smiles as he led Tom and me through some easy stretches before our run.

"Great job yesterday," he said.

"Way to go, Val!" Tom also said.

"Why am I not enjoying this or feeling as happy as you guys?" I asked.

Christopher smiled.

"I know that, despite the hard work, you're having some fun," he said.

"What do you mean *fun*?" I asked.

"I logged onto your Body Bugg info this morning and—"

"And what?" I asked.

"I saw an additional blip of late night activity."

"Yeah?" I said, not comprehending his point.

"Somebody was having fun," he said.

I blushed and turned to Tom, who read my eyes correctly. Christopher had been able to see that we had fooled around the night before. Tom's next thought was the same as mine. For weeks, Christopher had obviously been able to see those midnight work-outs that Tom had thought were a good idea. The guy, as sweet as he was, knew everything—and I mean *everything*—about me.

Maybe it was T.M.I.—even for me. It was for Tom, who looked at Christopher, wondering what else he might know. Then he turned toward me and said, "V, starting tonight, you take the Bugg off when we go to bed."

Notes to Myself

✿

A woman came up to me in the grocery store and said, "You look great." I said, "Thank you. I feel great." I realized that I had just explained the real goal of any diet—or any change of life for that matter.

Shopping is fun, not exercise—unless I walk faster. I don't know. . . . Any excuse to hit the shoe department.

I can't do anything about getting older. But I can do plenty about getting bored, complacent, and lazy—the things that make you feel old.

Tom came home the other day and noticed fresh flowers on the kitchen counter. "Who sent those?" he asked. No one, I explained. I bought them. Why not? I was loving myself.

Chapter Twenty-two

Size Doesn't Matter (It's How You Use Your Equipment)

For years, my brother, Patrick, and his wife Stacy have been king and queen of an annual Krewe of Helios parade in Arizona, a no-holds-barred Mardi Gras celebration at the end of their cul-de-sac involving pickup trucks festooned with balloons, beads, cold beer, pots of spicy gumbo, and platters of insanely delicious muffuletta sandwiches. After a couple of bites and beers, I'm transported from the desert to the French Quarter.

So when I saw the Evite to their party in my e-mail, I stared at it as if clicking on it would unleash a wicked computer virus. The timing sucked. Here I was on a mission to get rid of my muffin handles and all I could think about were her muffulettas. I RSVP'd anyway.

We went to their house the night before the party. As we helped them prepare, I showed Stacy my Bugg and explained that Tom and I planned to arrive toward the latter end of the party so that most of the food would be eaten. It was a surefire way to avoid temptation for someone who feared she had no willpower, which was my problem when I got around their Mardi Gras feast.

If there was any doubt, you only had to see me at that moment. As I gave her this lame excuse for missing half their party, I opened the silverware drawer, got out a spoon, flitted over to the stove, and began taste-testing the gumbo. Thankfully I was having only a couple of spoonsful. Previously, I wouldn't have been satisfied until I had consumed several bowls.

I can't say enough about Pat and Stacy's gumbo. My favorite part is that their recipe calls for the cook to drink a beer as it's prepared. Enough said, right?

Tom cleared his throat.

"How many weeks until you get in the bikini?" he asked.

"I'm just helping Stacy," I said.

"Helping?"

"I'm making sure it's good enough to serve," I said.

My brother saw me eyeing a bottle of Blair's 3 AM Death Sauce and said no way. Rarely does anything stand between me and a bottle of hot sauce, but thank goodness Patrick did. He saved me from getting into major trouble. The next day I would see their friend Dave lick the cork from the Death Sauce bottle on a dare— within seconds his forehead was covered in sweat.

"You saved my life," I said, jokingly.

Patrick didn't crack a smile.

"Val, it's even worse when it comes out," he said.

The highlight of arriving the day before to help them get ready came when I pulled up a chair to watch Stacy make her famous muffulettas. With my mouth watering, I was in lust as she brought out the sliced turkey, ham, and provolone cheese; then a large, hard salami; and then green and black olives; a dozen cloves of garlic; and a large jar of Italian giardiniera mix. At that point, I couldn't take it anymore. I told Tom to get me home.

As we were about to leave, I overheard Stacy telling my brother that their food processor was relatively small. I stopped by the front door.

"Guys, you've done this long enough to know that size doesn't matter," I said in a loud voice. "It's all about how you use the equipment you have."

I was one to talk. A few days later, after surviving Mardi Gras, I was back home, having my measurements taken. While my friend Kathy wrapped a tape measure around me, I stood in my kitchen with my arms raised and my inhibitions lowered. In the past, this would have been a scary proposition. In fact, I didn't know my exact measurements.

But I was participating in New York Fashion Week's annual Red Dress event, a charity show that raises awareness of heart disease as the leading killer of women and former *Project Runway* winner Christian Siriano was making a dress specially for me and needed my vital statistics. He he asked me to e-mail him my measurements. He said it casually, as if it was no big deal. And maybe it wasn't—to him. But I was, like, Hello, that's a scary thought—both taking my measurements and then putting them on the Internet. I did it, though, and without any second-guessing of the numbers. What was the big deal? I was doing a fashion show, not a centerfold.

Once in New York, I met with Christian and tried on the

dress. A camera crew from *Rachael Ray* followed me through the fitting. They captured my surprise when I saw that Christian had designed a strapless gown, a style that I had always avoided. Now, however, I was actually excited about breaking new ground for me in a fashion sense, and showing off my arms.

The belt Christian had made to go around my waist didn't fit. It was too small, because there were so many layers of fabric in the dress that they added another inch around the middle. I turned to the camera, winced, and said, "I didn't lie about my measurements. I swear."

I wore jeans and a T-shirt to rehearsals in the Bryant Park tent. As an actor, I know the benefits of rehearsal, but I thought that walking down the runway was a piece of cake and maybe a waste of time—that is until I heard someone mention that the point is to do it in high heels. I looked down at my feet. I had on Ugg boots. My heels were back in my hotel room. Oh, well, I wasn't trying to be Heidi Klum. I just wanted to do my part for the charity.

As it turned out, I did fine. I didn't fall, I smiled, and hopefully people thought Christian's dress was beautiful. Until I had reached the end of the runway, turned around, and begun walking back, I didn't realize that I was on the jumbo-sized screen. Of course, the view was of me walking away. In other words, all I saw was my ass.

Who ever sees that view of herself? I didn't know whether to stop, shriek, or run. What did I do? I reached around and grabbed my rear with both hands. I got a big laugh—and that made me feel great.

Back home, however, I sank into a funk. I had waltzed out of the glitzy part of my life and into a hornet's nest of real-life issues and obligations that needed my attention. Running on fumes and way too tired for my own good, I had been trying to do too much and had been saying yes to too many requests. Then I saw photographs of myself from the fashion show and thought I looked like a ton of lard compared to some of the other women who had participated. Suddenly, I was not myself.

None of the things that usually calmed me down worked. Even though I knew that the women to whom I was comparing myself had different body types, that some may have been unnaturally thin or unhealthy, it didn't matter.

My workouts suffered. Christopher knew that something was wrong, but I didn't feel like opening up to him.

Everyone goes through times when you feel out of sorts, or feel that the world is making too many demands and you just want to shut the door, be left alone, and feel sorry for yourself. I was having one of those times. I was angry, frustrated, tired, and I don't even know what all else.

It all came to a head one day when I attempted to install a hook in my closet where I wanted to hang my bathrobe, missed the nail, and hammered my thumb. I didn't laugh the way I had at Christmas when Tom had hammered his thumb while hanging lights outside. I had chided him then: the nail was right there. How could he possibly miss it?

For the answer, I didn't have to look any farther than my throbbing black-and-blue thumb. I had hit it because I was looking elsewhere, not at the nail. Likewise, I was off in the rest of my life because I wasn't looking at issues that I needed to address, including a miscommunication with my brother Patrick; a problem with Wolfie, who had ditched me for his dad after I had lectured him about not performing to expectations in some of his classes; and the continuing, pressing challenge of getting my body into a bikini.

I now had slightly less than a month to go and didn't feel anywhere near ready. I was really feeling the pressure now and was worried about the possibility of failure, which meant possibly disappointing a number of people, including myself.

At another time I might have shut myself in the house, not answered the phone, and let even the best-laid plans fall apart. But not now. Having made real progress over the past year of so-called maintenance, I recognized that I was letting the stress get to me and, in effect, cause all these different snags in my life. Instead of doing nothing, which would have been self-sabotage, I took action.

I called my brother; I reminded Wolfie via a text message that he had a mother who loved him whether he got an A in math or a C; and I had a long pep talk with Christopher, which got me back in sync. As I do frequently, I reminded myself that the maddeningly glorious imperfection of being merely human was the best that I could do in this lifetime.

In other words, sometimes you lose a sock in the dryer and sometimes you find it and make a pair. I could handle that reality. I knew it was better to deal with problems than let them linger.

Photos of me are always going to bug me, but I had to get over it and quit comparing myself to other women. There would always be someone who was happier, more together, richer, prettier, thinner, fitter, smarter, or more fabulous—and that didn't matter.

In the end, I decided to focus on my goals, watch my aim, and simply try to be the best version of me that I could be any given day.

Notes to Myself

✣

I realized that waking up groggy makes the start of the day move more slowly. So I stayed in bed an extra ten minutes after I woke up. But then I had to spring out of bed and sprint to the bathroom, and I realized that barely getting to the toilet makes the start of the day too fast for comfort.

Everyone tells me to drink more water. And they're right. Except not before bedtime.

I was working out in a hotel gym, and the man next to me was singing loud. I didn't even like the song. Three hours later that song was stuck in my head. There should be signs in the gym warning against iPod abuse.

I walked into the kitchen as Tom was giving Wolfie and Tony advice about women. It was cute. But he went on and on. I thought, Just tell them the essentials. Learn to say, "I love you," "I'm sorry, I was wrong" and "You're right honey."

Chapter Twenty-three

The Whole Muffuletta

After one more trip to New York, I faced Christopher for the first time in a week. We were in the entry hall, standing next to suitcases that Tom and I had left there the night before, too tired to drag them down the hall into the bedroom. I was holding a coffee cup, trying to generate some energy. My trainer was not pleased.

"How many more weeks till the commercial?" he asked.

"A little more than three," I said.

"And are you ready?"

I shook my head no.

He shook his head in response, as if to say you poor, pathetic procrastinator, it's time to get serious.

And then he simply said it:

"It's time to get serious. No more trips or travel until after the shoot."

"All right," I said.

"And no more alcohol," he added.

"It's Ash Wednesday," I said, "a perfect time to give up alcohol—until after the shoot."

I drew an imaginary line in the sand, just as when I had started my diet two years ago and vowed not to have a martini until I lost 25 pounds. I don't know what it is about me, but I need that type of mega challenge to get me up to the next level. With my back against the wall, I will muster a fierce determination and either reach my goal or go down in flames trying, and that's precisely where I was.

My weight was 131. Christopher said it was time to break through that barrier. He wanted me to aim for burning 3,000 calories a day. That meant twice-a-day workouts—once with him in the morning and then again by myself in the afternoon. Basically, if I was awake, I was working out. Wolfie would see me on the treadmill when he left for school, and I was usually on the Stairmaster when he came home.

"Oh, you're exercising again?" he would say. "What a surprise."

I thought that if I exercised more and ate even less I would lose more weight, and do it faster. But Christopher had me eat three meals a day plus a snack or two, because my body wouldn't function properly if I ate too little. Too few calories and it would start to shut down, or go into starvation mode, as it tried to hang on to the fuel that allowed it to perform properly. This regimen was about working hard but doing it in a healthy manner; it was to make me strong, not sick.

We had many illuminating talks about weight, nutrition, and fitness. We also talked about my body more than I had ever talked about it with anyone else. Christopher would get very specific about my arms or my thighs or some other body part. He looked at me like a sculptor. It was strange to focus so intently on my body since I had never been one of those actresses who steamed up the screen by taking off her clothes. Nor was I different in my personal life. But now, talking about my curves and abs and definition in my thighs was as natural as discussing the weather. Well, almost—

One day I was complaining that my butt seemed to defy all the miles I had logged and the weights I had lifted. It didn't look any smaller to me. With ten days to go before the shoot, I practically cried myself to sleep. I didn't think I could do it. I couldn't say why, whether it was my weight or I didn't feel right. My insecurity turned into negativity and snowballed. Christopher stopped it.

"You're tired," he said. "You're seeing things that aren't there."

"But I've had these problem areas since I was a kid," I argued.

"You are in amazing shape," he said.

"I am," I said.

"How do you feel?" he asked.

"Strong. Healthy."

"Then stop looking at yourself the way you did thirty-five years ago—or even three years ago. You're better than that."

On March 2, I confronted the enemy for the first time. Nancy, the woman who handles wardrobe for all my Jenny Craig commercials, brought over a number of bikinis. I hadn't put one of those suckers on in twenty-eight years, and I was reminded of why when I looked at myself in the first one I tried on. Again, I cried myself to sleep.

Nancy continued to bring more swimsuits, none of which worked. Complicating matters, I got my period—not real good for the self-esteem when trying on bathing suits. I was ready to shoot my scale—and anything else in my line of sight.

"If I had a gun," I said to Christopher.

"You'd see a Stairmaster and a treadmill with bullets in them," Tom said, "and one dead Sicilian."

My manager, Marc, was poised to call the whole thing off if I didn't feel 100 percent confident. Interestingly, he never asked me how I felt; instead he spoke to Tom, who had a better perspective on the situation. As they knew, no matter how tired, cranky, doubtful, or self-critical I sounded, I was too much of a team player ever to throw in the towel.

But mine wasn't the only opinion that mattered. Somehow word circulated among the Jenny Craig executives that I wasn't going to be ready for the shoot. Even though I didn't learn of this until later, I understood. They had a lot riding on this new campaign. Nervous, they called Christopher, who assured them that his star pupil would be ready.

Just over a week before the shoot, I finally broke the 130-pound mark. I got on the scale that morning and weighed 128 and change. The next day I was another pound lighter. It felt like I'd witnessed a miracle. I had no idea why; I hadn't done anything different. I'd just plugged away. Tom agreed. When he saw me trying on bikinis, he uttered a single word—"Wow."

A few days later, I was down three more pounds. This time I knew the reason. It had been water my body held on to while I was on my period. I laughingly hit myself on the side of my head as I got off the scale. Of course! Cue the *Rocky* music. I was going to do it.

Then the day got better. Nancy brought over a brand of bikini that I actually thought looked good on me. It was a basic, sporty Body Glove. I came out of the bedroom with a smile. Tom nodded.

"Yum," he said.

"Yum?" I replied. "How about *Thank God!*"

On Friday, three days before I left for Palm Springs, where the commercial was being shot, Christopher met with the director and his crew. The director told Christopher that he'd recently worked on a video with Madonna. He said that she had been in impossibly good shape, absolutely ripped, and he didn't want me to look like that. Given previous concerns only a few days earlier about whether I'd be ready, that was pretty funny.

"What did you tell him?" I asked Christopher when he told me about the meeting.

He laughed.

"I said, 'Okay, dude, I promise you Valerie Bertinelli will not look like Madonna.' "

I spent the weekend before the shoot at home by myself. Wolfie was with his dad, and Tom visited his children in Arizona. It was a good thing I was alone. I was able to focus on my workouts, the few errands I needed to run, and quiet time to keep my head in a calm place. On Sunday, I had a final fitting, and it went as everyone hoped. Even I was happy with the way I looked. I was ready.

On the day before the shoot, Christopher and I drove to the Parker Hotel in Palm Springs. Along the way, I checked in with Wolfie, who was at his dad's, and spoke to Tom, who was driving in from Arizona. My parents were also making their way to the Parker for a commercial that my mom was doing with Tom and me after I finished in the bikini.

Now that the big event was finally here, I was in a positive mindset. I felt good about all the hours I had put in; it was like being ready for a big game. Christopher and I reminisced about my progress over the months we had trained together. He noted that running and working out had become a part of my life, not something I only did for the photo shoot. I didn't disagree.

For much of the drive, I was surprisingly mellow. I stayed quiet and confident in my head and pictured myself sipping celebratory champagne when we were finished, though I didn't want to get too far ahead of myself.

At the hotel, I waited briefly for Tom to arrive, and then we walked the hotel's lush grounds, which were bursting with spring flowers. I enjoyed the perfumed desert air. Tom praised me for being relaxed. I didn't know if I was calm or intensely focused, but I did admit to being immensely pleased and even impressed with the shape I had gotten myself into.

"God bless Christopher," I said.

My positive attitude earned an affectionate whoop from Tom. All the hours of sweat were worth every ounce of pain, and hopefully the complaints weren't too much to bear. For the first time in my life, I actually liked my arms. I also liked seeing a line in my thighs from all the squats. I had done the best I could with my butt. I had a shapely body and no amount of diet or exercise could change that fact. And that's okay. I didn't want to look like a little boy from behind. I had curves.

I remembered back when I used to say to myself, God, if I could just stay under 150 pounds I'll be fine. And I had trouble getting there. Now, I had planted a stake in the ground at 132, but my new goal was to live between 124 and 129. It felt normal and realistic for me, at almost forty-nine years old.

Mention of the word maintenance brought a laugh. I had maintained, and then some. I had improved. I was fit, and loved being strong and healthy. I felt like anything was possible. I could scale a mountain or run a marathon if I wanted. I had confidence in myself and my body, another new sensation for me.

I wouldn't ever feel 100 percent at ease about being in a bikini, not at my age, but my bikini body was attainable, not one of those scary, sculpted, impossible bodies that make you go, Why bother trying? I was comfortable in my own skin. I hoped that would show more than anything else.

After a light dinner, we went back to the room, and Jen, my spray-tan artist, came over. She had me take off all my clothes—and I mean all of them—and stand on the back patio. Then she sprayed me to within an inch of my Italian grandfather's color. It was a bit of a thrill. I was finally naked, and the most gratifying thing about it was that it was exactly as I'd always hoped. I liked what I saw—but I felt even better.

Strangely, I had no qualms about standing buck naked outside and in almost plain view. That is if you knew where to look—or got lucky, which was possible. Only a 5-foot wall and a small, flat, square umbrella hid me from hotel guests walking across the courtyard as they returned to their room from the bar or dining room.

"Tom, I'm on the patio—naked," I said.

"Can you be quiet, please," he said.

"With another woman!"

Jen just laughed.

Fearful that I might provide someone with a cheap thrill, I had Tom go outside and station himself in front of the patio wall to make sure no one stopped and looked. In reality, he said hi to everyone who passed by, which caused them to stop and probably wonder who was chirping about being naked on a patio.

Finally, I gave him the all-clear sign. I shouted, "Honey, it's okay. I'm no longer standing naked on the balcony!"

"Good to know," he replied. "Thanks for telling *everyone*."

Notes to Myself

At some point I quit asking God to help get me through my run. Instead I thanked Him at the end for letting me make it all the way.

Here's the tip: think of every step in a workout as a step in the right direction.

Wolfie texted me good luck and said he loved me. I really did feel lucky.

Chapter Twenty-four

Another Fifteen Minutes

I started the next day at 5 a.m. in the hotel gym, shooting B-roll of my workout for *Oprah*. For the first time in several months, I had trouble exercising. I had hit a wall mentally and physically. Nevertheless, I pushed myself and got through one more workout. There was a bright spot. I weighed a feathery 122 pounds. Tom snapped a picture of the scale.

After cleaning up, we went to the set. The commercial was being shot at a private mansion about ten minutes from the hotel. Calling it a mansion doesn't do it justice. Situated on an acre of land at the base of one of the mountains, the sprawling home featured at least five swimming pools of different sizes and shapes. Upon our arrival, we joined everyone else and walked around in awe. It was like stepping into another reality.

For all the work that had gone into getting ready for the commercial, the shoot itself was a simple process. Anticlimactic is probably a better description. There were three parts to it. The first segment featured me in a robe, talking about how I used to dread summers. In the second, I wore a one-piece swimsuit. Finally, in the third I wore a bikini.

By the third part, I was ready to be finished. You would think my unveiling would have been a big deal, but it was more of an anticlimax to months of worry and hard work. I stood around in that two-piece as if I went to work dressed like that every day. Though I felt slightly naked, I told myself, as I had the day before, be naked. I blocked out the cameras, the crew, and the rest. I had one moment where I thought about asking if it was really necessary to have so many extras standing right behind me, looking at my ass. But I could live with them seeing my cellulite.

That's right, I was able to shrug off my cellulite. I see plenty of teenage girls on the beach with fat-free bodies and think good for you. See you in thirty years. Do I wish I didn't have cellulite? Yes. Does it make me self-conscious in a bathing suit? Sure it does. But do I look better now? Definitely. And I can deal with that. It's one more reminder that I'm not perfect.

But that's okay. I'm not supposed to be perfect. I'm supposed to be me, my best me possible—and that's what I hoped would come across on the commercial.

Once we finished, I allowed myself an enormous sigh of relief. I heard applause and then was congratuated by Tom, Christopher, my managers, the Jenny Craig people, the director, and my parents. My dad, as he'd done since I was a kid on *One Day at a Time*, told me that I looked terrific, like his Gina Lollobrigida, which was what he had always called me. I laughed to myself, knowing that earlier my hairstylist, Roque, had gone for a Sophia Loren look.

After a break for lunch, we regrouped and shot a second commercial. This one starred my mom and Tom. Back in December, I had promised her we would do another commercial after she recovered from her chest infection. Now, as I watched her climb on the back of a big Harley motorcycle with Tom, I was prouder of her than I was of myself. They really did roar off as I said, "Hey, Mom, where're you going with my boyfriend?" Inside, I was thinking, "You go, girl!" Ironically enough, it was the same thing she had said to me.

At the end of the day, I let out a celebratory whoop and we broke out the prosecco. The next day, I went for a three-and-a-half-mile run with Tom, and amazingly enough, I loved it. Then we shot two more commercials and I met about my upcoming *Oprah* appearance and *People* magazine shoot. That night, Jack, Marc, Nancy, and Kacie (my wardrobe gals), Tom, and I went out for Mexican food. Even though the pressure was off, I didn't go crazy. I only had a handful of chips and left more margarita in my glass than I drank.

With Christopher's help, I had changed. Something had clicked inside me. Indeed, Tom and I stayed in Palm Springs for a few days after the shoot, and we began our weekend with a long run down the city's main drag, once again running for fun, not because it was a means to an end. Now it was my life. It was something positive and healthy for myself. A new part of my life had started.

On Tuesday, March 17, I flew to Chicago and taped *Oprah* the next day. She was kind and sweet and gave me major props, but one of her two new cocker spaniel puppies had died over the weekend and the other was sick, so she was stoic and just trying to get through the day. I was on the set for maybe five minutes. I returned home that afternoon and three days later shot the cover of *People*.

We took the photos on the beach in Malibu. It was 57 degrees outside, way too cold to be prancing on the beach in next-to-nothing. But I smiled through the shoot, and then happily and eagerly exhaled. I was finally done with this monster I'd created from an itty-bitty bikini—or so I thought.

Less than a week later, I was getting myself a second cup of coffee and half-listening to the *Today* show. Before going to a commercial, they teased the next segment, showing a magazine cover with the face blurred out. Over it, one of the hosts asked something like, "Which former child star posed in a bikini at age forty-eight and looks this hot!" Suddenly I paid more attention. I caught the tail-end of the shot and thought, what? That can't be me.

The magazine wasn't supposed to be out for another week. But sure enough, when the show returned from the break I saw myself on the magazine's cover, standing with one hand on my hip, in my bikini. I blurted out, "Holy sh—" Tom came in and saved me from having a minor coronary, as well as eye damage. My face was nearly inside the TV, trying to get a close-up view.

At first I was a little disappointed in the choice they made. I didn't think it was the best photo we took that day. But I understood the picture. My face clearly expressed a feeling of astonishment, as if you could hear the little voice in my head say, "I can't believe I'm doing this." In fact, they ran that quote on the cover: "I can't believe I did it." And it was absolutely true. Even in the days and weeks after, I still couldn't believe it.

I knew that being on the cover in a bikini would generate some attention, but it was hard believe what a big deal it actually became. All of the TV entertainment shows led their broadcasts with the story. Both the *New York Post* and *Daily News* ran full-sized photos. I also landed on Perez Hilton's website, which made me laugh. The man barely knew that I existed. My status in his celebrity-filled world was so low that he called me a Z-lister.

"I don't know whether to be excited or horrified," I exclaimed to my managers, Jack and Marc, who updated me on the spreading buzz.

"Excited," they said. "It's great."

"But aren't there more important stories?" I asked. "I mean we have an African-American president facing two wars, Wall Street has screwed with our financial system, the car industry where my dad spent his entire career is in free fall, newspapers are going out of business. . . . and we're talking about a forty-eight-year-old woman in a bikini?"

"Yes, we are," they said.

"Don't get me wrong," I continued. "I'm pleased—actually I'm amazed that people are still interested. It's weird."

I went through a gamut of emotions. For a day or two, I was on a strange high from all the compliments and attention. How could I not be a little swept away? Then I got mildly annoyed and even a little amused at speculation that my picture had been retouched and reshaped to look bikini-ready. I understood why people wondered. If it hadn't been me on the cover, I probably would have been like a lot of other people and asked how could she possibly look like that?

I assumed the *People* magazine's photo editors had applied the usual amount of air-brushing to smooth out my skin, eliminate a wrinkle or two, any pimples, and even out the color. But I was not photoshopped in any way, shape, or form.

That weekend the magazine hit the stands, Wolfie flew to see his girlfriend. He hadn't said anything to me about the *People* cover yet. However, when he called from the airport to let me know he'd made it to Liv's, I asked if he'd noticed anything interesting as he walked through the terminal.

"Like on a magazine?" I hinted.

"Oh, yeah, Ma," he said. "You were everywhere. You looked good."

His lack of enthusiasm kept me real. In fact, I quickly got to the point where I felt the attention was enough, more than enough. I began to point out women on other magazine covers who looked much better, who really had knockout bodies, like Jenny McCarthy, Cameron Diaz, and Halle Berry. They are physical marvels. To a certain extent, you have to be born with those genes.

However, mine is the body that anybody could have if she watched her diet and worked out long and hard enough. My point through this whole deal has been that my transformation from fat to fit to fitter is available to anyone who wants it. I think people got the message. But again, it was almost too much for me to handle.

Toward the end of the week, I went into a depression—a deep, dark, sorry-assed funk. I tumbled down into a hole where I moped my way through the day. I couldn't believe what a wimp I was being. I didn't understand it. Tom was incredibly patient and understanding. He kept his distance until I needed to talk, then he listened and gently helped me see that I was exhausted. I'd worked nonstop every day for nearly a month, with my entire being focused on a single goal. Quite simply, I'd run out of gas, physically, mentally, and emotionally.

I walked around wondering what was wrong and asking myself what was next. My voice echoed through my head, *Now what?*

I had a sense that I might have upset the natural balance of my life. It was like a bad joke or metaphysical *Punk'd* episode. I'd had my fifteen minutes of fame, and now I was having another fifteen minutes. I thought you only got one. What was going on? It made me worry. Too much niceness was coming at me again. Too many good things were happening. As was my tendency, I prepared for the other shoe to drop.

"It's just been a bizarre month," I told Tom as I tapped out an e-mail at the computer.

I was in my bathrobe. He had come back from a short run and was gulping down a glass of juice.

"You need to rest," he said. "You're being beaten down by your emotions. Maybe you're getting sick from stress. It's like a rubber band snapping. You were pulled so tight. Something has to give."

He was right. A moment later, I broke. I burst into tears—and with that rush of water came a torrent of fears and frustrations. Exhausted and sick, I stayed in bed for a couple of days, blew my nose, and let the dust settle. I felt like I was a fraud. Even after a couple of years as a Jenny Craig spokesperson, I wasn't accustomed to being associated with being fit or in shape. That wasn't in my resume. I worried the focus was too much on my body. I wanted the message to be a more inspirational one about getting through the issues in your life and coming out better, stronger, and wiser.

"What makes you think it's not inspirational?" asked Tom.

I didn't have an answer. He reminded me of the picture that magazines and newspapers had run of a shirtless Obama on the beach in Hawaii. He said the President might have been surprised people would care about something as trite as him walking out of the surf in a bathing suit. On the other hand, who could argue there was something inspirational about seeing a nearly forty-eight-year-old man in his position looking fit and enjoying his family?

While over time I would come to agree with Tom, I still had to get over one final hurdle, the one that made me feel that I needed to head for the basement before the storm hit.

Deep down, I didn't feel like—or I should more accurately say a part of me didn't feel like—I deserved the good things that were happening to me. It's why I felt like a great big phony as I lay in bed, wallowing in a pool of snot and sorrow. It's why I'd sabotaged moments in my past and failed to enjoy some of the good times to the fullest. It's why I'd always regained the weight I'd lost on previous diets.

But as I talked over these fears with Tom, I realized they no longer rang true. My words had neither substance nor sincerity. After all that I'd accomplished, I couldn't take these old thought habits seriously. Good things do happen to me and others for a reason. We make them happen. My weight loss was real. I'd kept the weight off for more than a year. That was real, too. I'd also gotten into the best shape of my life, and more importantly I was getting my whole life into its best shape.

Instead of worrying whether I deserved these things, I told myself to appreciate them and be grateful, to take it all in and recognize that it felt good, that I felt good—and that was, after all, the goal. I'd made a conscious decision to feel this way and I'd worked my butt off to get there.

"Why not enjoy life while you can?"

My mom said that, not me. She called as I was shaking off my cold, emerging from my depression, and getting back into the flow of normal, daily life. She and my dad were leaving the following

Tuesday on a cruise to Hawaii. She was excited. It had been almost six months to the day since she had gotten sick on a cruise in the Caribbean. She had no fears about going away again. She couldn't wait to get back on the ship.

"I'm ready to eat and drink and dance," she said.

"Good for you, Mom," I said. "Have a drink for me and toast you and Dad. You're my inspiration. I want to be like you when I grow up."

Notes to Myself

✤

I ate the chocolate on my pillow and had sweet dreams.

Whatever I revealed by getting into a bikini was only a fraction of what I revealed to myself before I ever tried it on.

Keep your eye on the goal. But you won't find it looking down at the scale. You have to look inside your heart, look up for inspiration, and look out at the rest of your life . . .

What you concentrate upon you bring into your life.—Emmet Fox

But he who endures to the end will be saved.—Matthew 24:13

Chapter Twenty-five

My Grandmother's Soup

I wanted to get away for my birthday, someplace low-key and close to home, which was how we arrived at Laguna. I was eager to shed the stress of the past year once and for all and start forty-nine on a high, and full of anticipation of a great year.

One peek inside my suitcase provided my entire agenda. I brought one dress, two swimsuits, lots of workout clothes, and even more lingerie. As was my habit now, I hit the hotel's gym, which overlooked the ocean. Time melted away as I stared at the water while doing cardio on the treadmill. I let negative thoughts about myself and those against whom I harbored grudges empty into the waves, and I reminded myself to embrace the good in my life and the world.

If I sound more meditative and serene than usual, so be it. Blame the setting. The vast stretch of blue in front of me and the rhythmic sound of the waves as they crashed on the shore had a calming effect. The ocean was big, grand, beautiful, and timeless. It had fueled adventures, inspired dreams and poems, and nourished life. It put my tiny grievances into perspective and filled me with awe and wonder. I appreciated being able to stand there and gawk and think.

I said a prayer of thanks. I felt my soul rise with the lightness of being that I had wanted when I first set out to lose weight, except now I knew it didn't have anything to do with weight. I was taken back to when Tom and I had gone into St. Patrick's, and I had sat there wondering why I didn't understand anything the priest was saying, feeling as though something must be wrong with me, and then finally staring at a clean square in the ceiling as if it were a window into the next place I needed to go.

And so it was. I just didn't figure it out until now, in the gym, when I realized that special connection to God that I had always thought resided in a church wasn't there. It was inside me. Going to church helps some people find it. But there are other ways, too. The point is to find it, and then believe it.

When I was in St. Patrick's, it was as if God had been trying to say, "I'm glad you like the architecture. But look around, here and outside and most importantly inside yourself. I'm everywhere."

After our three nights in Laguna, I made sure my daily life included the activities that made me feel healthy. I walked, worked out, ate good food, read, and talked openly to Tom about the good moments and the things that confused me. Christopher began talking about getting me to run a marathon. I looked at him like he had lost his mind. Then again, I had given him that same look before and I knew what had happened then.

"We'll start with a 5K," he said, rubbing his hands together enthusiastically.

"Yeah, right," I said, though after a brief pause, I asked, "How many calories does that burn? I mean, maybe. . . ."

I don't dismiss anything that might make me feel better about myself. Don't tell that to my pal, Rachael Ray, whose invitation to jump out of an airplane with her I have repeatedly declined. Other than that, I am open to most new ideas and adventures that will keep me on the track of self-improvement. These thoughts can still surprise me, but for the most part this openness and effort are what I had hoped for, and indeed needed, to figure out when I started on maintenance.

Everyone knows how to lose weight. We are very good at it, in fact. Our problem is that practically none of us knows how to keep the weight off.

Hopefully, I have been able to change that through my own experiences by showing that losing weight is just the first step in a long-range process of evolution and transformation. After you hit your weight goal, you need to work on the rest of your life—and I mean work on it. It doesn't end. Maintenance isn't just for the rest of your life. It *is* the rest of your life.

I am flattered and moved by all the lovely women who say that I have inspired them. The truth is, *they* inspire *me*. It's the best part of my journey. We are a circle that keeps one another moving forward. As I have had to keep telling myself, none of us is perfect. We are going to have good days and bad days, some that are easy and some that are full of temptation. All you can do is try your best.

To make life easier, I suggest following these simple guidelines: Eat sensibly and in small portions. Exercise daily. Face problems when they arise. Believe that you do deserve good things, and work hard to get them. Also, don't pretend you have twelve items or fewer in your grocery cart so you can get into the express line. If you lie about the little things, you are apt to lie about the bigger things, too. Hey, I'm going to go out on a limb and say, if you have a full basket and see someone with only a couple of items, let her go ahead of you. It's a good thing. The more kind gestures we make, the better off all of us will be. It's like getting flowers on your birthday—you can never have too many.

In June, my parents and my brother Patrick and his wife, Stacy, came to Los Angeles for Wolfie's high school graduation. I got very emotional watching the kids I had known since kindergarten and first grade stand on stage and make speeches, sing songs, and accept that piece of paper ushering them to the next stage of their life. Ed and I traded glances through the ceremony, the sort of looks that asked, "Remember when. . . ." Of course we did, and were grateful for all those memories.

Wolfie was adorable. After seeing him texting someone on his phone, I sent him a text of my own, asking what he was texting. He put his phone away. At night, we celebrated around a fire at the beach. My parents seemed relaxed for the first time in a long while, and as they recounted the terrific time they'd had on their cruise, I couldn't help from tapping my mom on the shoulder and saying, "I told you so."

Toward the end of the month, I heard the same thing from Christopher after we completed my first 5K run in Culver City. I crossed the finish line in 28:49, the fifth fastest time among women in my age group who ran that race. After getting over that I had finished, I immediately began thinking I could do better.

Later, when Christopher brought up a half marathon, I didn't dismiss the idea. Instead, I asked when it was.

I am past making predictions. I want to feel that the best is still ahead. As my mom has said, You never know. One night, with Wolfie and Tony sleeping at Ed's, Tom and I found ourselves with nothing to do. We decided to have dinner at Mozza Osteria, a popular Italian restaurant in West Hollywood that requires reservations weeks in advance. As we expected, it was packed when we got there, so we sat at the counter and I ordered the tortellini in brodo soup. As soon as I tasted the first spoonful, I stopped talking. I stopped everything, in fact, and stared in frozen disbelief at Tom, who asked what was going on. I tasted the soup again.

"Oh, my God," I said. "The soup."

"What?" he asked. "Is something wrong?"

"No, it's incredible, "I said. "I can't believe it. This soup tastes exactly like my grandmother's cappelletti soup."

Tom tasted a spoonful and agreed that it was delicious.

"Really good," he said.

"It's not *good*," I said. "It's phenomenal. It's magical. I've spent forty years trying to find a soup that tastes like this."

"Enjoy it."

"I am," I said. "I swear, it's like I've been transported back into my Aunt Adeline and Uncle Dino's basement in Delaware."

I finished the soup and set my spoon down with a clink in the empty bowl. I was okay with the spiritual and personal connection not lasting longer than it did. I was grateful for having found the soup and enjoyed being able to remember feelings that were fundamental to my life. Some people find timeless connections in church. Others meditate. It seems fitting to me that I would have my own religious experience in a bowl of rich buttery broth with pasta.

I didn't look for explanations or validation. All I know is what I told Tom after dinner.

"We're coming back."

Final Note to Myself

✌

I have family, health, and love. . . . I don't need to get on a scale to know that I am succeeding in maintenance.

What next?

My GED . . . seriously.

And even though I can't believe I'm jotting this down, it looks like it might be a marathon. Ack!

Acknowledgments

As this book makes evident, my life is full of family, friends, and business associates who have helped shape me in countless ways and continue to teach me lessons every day. I am blessed to have all of you in my life.

As I said several times in these pages, I don't know what I have done to be this fortunate, but I'll take it and hope I give some of the same back to all of you.

Likewise, I want to extend the same gratitude to all the kind people who I have met at book signings or who stop me in stores and restaurants and tell me that I have inspired or motivated them to lose weight or get in better shape. You don't have to say, "Excuse me, I'm sorry to bother you," It's not a bother. We're all in this together!

Todd, what in God's name would I do without you? Are you sure you're not really me? A better, funnier, faster version? Next time we do this I want more time for the fun part, okay? Stop rolling your eyes. Love to you, Beth, and your beautiful children.

ACKNOWLEDGMENTS

Mom and Dad, as a parent myself, I know it's not always easy, and so I know it wasn't easy with me, but thanks for putting up with me and showing me that love continues to bloom.

Pat, Stacy, David, Drew, Laura, Calvin, Bailey, and my cherished Vispi and Fairweather famiglia, when you read this please take a moment and shut your eyes and imagine me giving you a hug.

Tony, Andie, Angela, and Dom, you have enriched my life in too many ways to mention. You're great kids and it's a treat watching you grow up.

Anthony and Helen Vitale, thank you for trusting me with your son. You like me better though, right?

Angela, you're the sister I never knew I wanted. I'm truly blessed to know you. And to the rest of the Vitale, O'Leary, Altieri, Palmisano famiglia, I wish we could see each other more often, but I'll take what I can get, grazie!

Christopher, I have cursed you, kissed you, and just plain been amazed by you. You aren't a trainer; you're an artist who understands that you can't reshape the outside if you don't also work on the inside. And Colin, thank you, you're the perfect cheerleader, for T, Chris, and me.

Jack and Marc, my longtime managers, you guys are my version of Butch Cassidy and the Sundance Kid, killers (with great taste and judgment) masquerading as Paul Newman and Robert Redford. And don't ask me which is which.

Heidi and Jill at PMK/HBH, you both have such patience, grace, and beauty. Thank you for taking care of me.

Jonathan, Nevin, and everyone at Innovative Artists, thank you again for believing in me.

Jamie, Barry, and all at Jackoway Tyerman Wertheimer Austen Mandelbaum Morris & Klein, thank you for everything.

Lois, Craig, Rod, Karin, Amanda, Charlotte and everyone at Gelfand, Rennert & Feldman, Thank you for all your hard work. Miss you, Gabby.

Terry, Kathy and Abra, No one finer could be in charge. It will be so!

Nancy, Kacie, Roque, Jetty, Torston, Carol, Bruce, Cristoph, Linda, Chandra, Daniela, and Jen at Portofino, thank you for making me feel beautiful.

Phil and Jimmy, still in my life, gratefully so.

To Dan Strone at Trident Media Group, who knew? I guess you did. Thank you.

To Leslie Meredith, Donna Loffredo, and everyone at Free Press, I know that, although writing may look like an individual endeavor, it's really a team sport and with you, I couldn't have better teammates. Thank you.

To Jenny Craig, I want you to know that very often during tough times, when more than anything I want to stuff gobs of food in my face, I stop and ask, "WWJCD—what would Jenny Craig do?" You are an inspirational woman.

To all of my buds at Jenny Craig Headquarters, okay, you got me in a bikini and I have to admit, it wasn't that bad. So, what next? A topless beach in the South of France? Just kidding (about the topless part). Thank you for everything. Truly.

To my girlfriends, the book club ladies, and the small, intimate group of women (and their husbands) with whom I have laughed, cried, driven carpools, sat next to at graduations, and traded notes about our kids on the phone, I will simply say I couldn't have asked for warmer or wiser friends. Again, I don't know what I did to be so fortunate to have all of you in my life, but I'll take it. Let's keep going!

To Ed and Janie, I say, Mazel Tov! I want to wish you a long and happy and healthy marriage.

Tom, I said it at the beginning of this book, but I'll say it again: Thanks for finding me. Without you, I doubt I would have started on my own journey to finding it. More than that, you ran a half marathon with me. That is love and I love you!

Wolfie, no project has inspired me more than being a mother. Nor has any project presented as many challenges or as much joy. I will forever feel so honored and blessed to be your mother. Could you do me one favor, though? Please pick up your towels! I love you, to the moon and back—and more.

About the Author

VALERIE BERTINELLI has been acting since the age of twelve, appearing in more than two dozen made-for-TV movies. She is most recognized for her appearances on the long-running sitcom, *One Day at a Time,* and more recently on *Touched by an Angel.* Now a spokesperson for Jenny Craig, Bertinelli was born in Wilmington, Delaware, and raised in Southern California, and was married for twenty years to Eddie Van Halen (they split up in 2001). Currently she lives in Los Angeles.